Have the Guts to Do it Right

Raising Grateful and Responsible Children
In an Era of Indulgence

Sheri Moskowitz Noga, M.A.

To Eric and Lily
and the joy of raising you

Acknowledgments

I am grateful to a variety of people for the help, love, and support I've been given in writing this book. To Dee Vickers and Autumn J. Conley for editing, Liz Saelzler for content suggestions, and of course, Dan Noga for believing in what I had to say. To Leslie Pielack and Dr. Susan Darlington Elwert for their devoted assistance in my personal and professional development. This book wouldn't have been written without them.

And to all the people who have shown me kindness and reached out when I needed a hand, I am grateful. It is through your generosity that my faith in humanity has been sustained.

A Note to Readers

The names of those persons used in this book are fictitious. Any identifying characteristics which could identify clients have been altered in order to protect their privacy and confidentiality. The dialogue represents either the gist of what was said or a representation of it. The information contained in this book is intended for educational purposes only. It should not be used as a substitute for psychological and/or medical consultation with a competent health care professional. This book's contents may be used as an adjunct to a rational and responsible healthcare program prescribed by a healthcare practitioner. It is not intended as psychotherapy, a diagnosis, prescription or treatment of any health disorder

Readers are to understand that this book is designed to assist them in understanding their relationships with their children and their own styles of parenting. This book provides guidelines for improving parents' relationships with their children. The reader accepts sole responsibility for the decisions made the results and the consequences regarding their use of this material. The authors and publishers are in no way liable for any misuse of the material.

Table of Contents

"Love and work are the cornerstones of our humanness."

Sigmund Freud

"Be kind whenever possible. It is always possible."

The Dalai Lama

Preface

It's a clear and bright blue day in New York City in early autumn. I'm waiting in line outside a popular restaurant in Chinatown when a couple in their thirties emerges with their little girl, no older than three. At first glance it is obvious that these are attentive and loving parents. I watch as they pull out a stroller and say to their child, "Do you want to get in?" I can tell by the way they are asking that they want her to cooperate so they can proceed with their day. Their daughter can also tell that this is what they want. She shakes her head 'no', and the negotiation begins. Both parents spend several minutes trying to explain to her why she should get in the stroller. They can't move on until she does as the streets are crowded and she is too small.

After awhile the father goes into a tea shop next to the restaurant. They have resigned themselves to this being a long process. The mother continues to patiently talk with her child about why she should get into the stroller. Inevitably, the little girl becomes agitated and starts to cry, dissolving into a tantrum. She can't overcome her own resistance to cooperating, and the situation won't move forward. I'm wondering how this dilemma will resolve when my name is called and I go inside.

* * *

My husband and I are watching the sunset at Tunnel Park in western Michigan. It is one of my favorite places in the world. As we walk through the small passenger tunnel that opens onto an expansive view of Lake Michigan, I see a woman in her forties taking photos of her teenage son. Her husband stands by, observing and making comments. I hear him start to get angry; something in the process isn't going the way he thinks it should. He starts getting madder and louder, saying something about how embarrassed he is by his son's behavior. I'm confused because I haven't witnessed anything going wrong. They turn to leave through the tunnel and suddenly the man starts loudly swearing and yelling at the boy, then hauls off and hits him hard in the back of the head. There are many people around and everyone can clearly hear and see what is happening. No one is saying anything.

As they walk behind me through the tunnel, I turn around and yell, "Hey! Stop that!" There is no response from them or anyone else. The man's screaming is intensifying as they are retreating into the darkness; he is being extremely loud and swearing unabashedly at his son. Again he reels back and hits him in the head, very hard. I yell louder, "Stop hitting him! Stop it!" My husband then yells, "You're a fool!"

Like a scene from a bad film the man turns toward us in the dark and barks, "What did you say? I won't hit a woman, but I'll hit a man, you (expletive, expletive, expletive)." He starts marching back through the tunnel and I begin to panic, fearing my husband is about to be assaulted. The man, accompanied by his son, comes right up to my husband and jabs his finger within an inch of his nose over and over, making threatening and derogatory remarks. I'm relieved to see he has enough self-control not to hit him. His son joins in the reverie, chiming, "Yeah! He's just disciplining his kid!" The bully then turns to me and repeats the same performance. I'm struck by how emerald green his eyes are as well as by my own calm in the face of his rage. Years of work as a psychotherapist have served me well; I'm comfortable with intense emotion as long as I'm not in physical danger.

Eventually the man and his son retreat back through the tunnel. His wife is nowhere to be seen, staying out of the way at the other end. Although we are surrounded by many people who have come to enjoy the sunset as we have, no one says a word to us. No one has phoned the police.

* * *

My decision to write this book has come from a multitude of experiences inside and outside of my office, watching parents from one end of the spectrum to the other who have no idea how to manage their children. Most of the clients who come to see me are not monstrous like the man cited above. Most are well-intentioned, informed adults who are parenting in the best way they know how. They can't understand, then, why their children have ended up behaving and feeling so badly and why their families are in such turmoil.

These parents don't understand that loving their children and making them the center of their universe is not a formula for happiness. These parents have acted in accordance with their peers, watched how other parents indulge their children and then followed suit. The clients who come to my office provide their children with the same level of material goods and opportunities they see in families around them. Their devotion to their children's happiness is complete.

It seems almost no one is available to tell these parents that in giving their children everything and expecting little from them, they are spoiling not only their children but also their children's ability to enjoy life in the future. Parents come to therapy desperate for help in understanding their family's unhappiness, without any understanding of how their and their children's lives have gotten so bad.

Most of these parents are not that difficult to help. Often, all they need is support in following their own gut instincts, which tell them they are not appropriately parenting. Most mothers and fathers who come to see me have a sense that they are overindulging their children and allowing behaviors they shouldn't. They seem to need my permission to expect more of their children and to act as the authority figures that they are. With some minimal guidance many of these parents are able to make simple changes in their approach with their children and get rapid, positive results.

I have felt compelled to write this book as a means of guiding parents who simply need support to do what's right. Our culture has fallen sadly short of encouraging appropriate authoritative behaviors in parents. From television shows about nannies coming to the rescue of crazed families to dog training boot camps for undisciplined pets, we've become a culture out of control, unable to exert influence even within our own families.

Being a good parent takes heart <u>and</u> guts. I hope what I've written will help you discover the inner, loving authority figure your child needs you to be. Raising a healthy child requires love and discipline. My intention in writing down much of what I tell clients in my office every day is to offer a professional opinion in support of loving and adequate parenting, which will help produce content and purposeful children. If you have the guts to have a child in the first place, you hopefully have the guts to want to do it right

A Culture of Indulgence

Our country is in crisis on many fronts. The desire for immediate gratification and a lack of self-control have led to huge problems in the areas of finance, food, weight and fidelity. Likewise, indulging our children has led to a marked increase in the incidence of narcissism among the younger generation. These young people show a decreased ability to empathize with others as well as feelings of emptiness, depression and poor self-esteem.

I have been a psychotherapist in private practice for thirty years. During that time, I have treated many families, children, adolescents and couples struggling with how to get along with each other and in the world. For the past fifteen or more years, I, along with many of my colleagues, have noticed a disturbing trend in what brings children and families into our offices. Increasingly we are seeing children who are out of control, disrespectful, entitled and confused, children who seem to feel 'empty' and parents who are helpless to do anything about it. Race, religion, and social standing seem to have nothing to do with these difficulties. It appears to be all about our culture of indulgence, entitlement and lack of self-control.

How many parents have I heard say the following:
* "My child's behavior/mouth is out of control and we don't know what to do about it."

* "We try to discipline them but it doesn't work, we tell them to go to their room, but they won't go!"

* "My child isn't able to accept 'no' as an answer to anything they want."

* "They have uncontrollable fits if they don't get their way."

* "My kids fight with each other constantly, they are driving us crazy."

How many of these children have broken down into tears alone with me in my office, expressing self-loathing for their lack of control?   In even greater numbers, I see kids of all ages who seem lost, who don't understand what makes life worthwhile and often express distaste for work and have trouble with social relationships. These kids also increasingly can't see things from their parents' perspectives and view them as irrelevant.

What parents don't seem to realize is that indulging their children's bad behaviors and attitudes makes these same kids feel terrible about themselves. It's hard to count the number of children who have made statements to me like, "My parents give me whatever I want" (one fourteen-year-old girl said as she showed me her Tiffany diamond earrings), or "My mom and dad aren't good at enforcing limits they set on me" (said by an eighteen-year-old that had dropped out of college and was living at home for free, with no expectations of him finding work). Their parents are almost always shocked to hear how guilty and self-hating these children feel because they often don't reveal this in front of them.

The reality I see in my office is that these kids know their behaviors, expectations and problematic emotions are off base. They are lost, flailing, and floundering. Some of them show their distress outwardly with tantrums, out-of-control verbiage, aggression toward siblings and more. Others turn their distress inward and report behaviors such as cutting, despair, and drug and alcohol use.

There are those children who do express remorse to their parents but continue their same out-of-control behaviors the next day or even the next hour. As much as they have a conscience and awareness of the inappropriateness of their behavior, they can't seem to get a handle on it.

How is it that parents and children have lost their way to such a degree? And how can they be helped? Often the parents coming to see me have seen other therapists who have been unable to help them or their child. I have heard stories of children being treated with cognitive behavioral therapy, psychoanalysis, medication, and countless other methods to no avail. These parents are in a state of combined desperation and depression, believing their situation can't be fixed. They come into my office well intended, wanting direction and willing to work to make changes.

Then there are the parents who bring their children to therapy with the expectation that the therapist will 'fix' their child. They often don't want to be involved in the treatment, except for providing transportation and payment. These parents become anxious or angry if they are expected to look at themselves and make changes in how they relate to their kids.

There are also parents who say they are willing to work on themselves in order to help their children but who, in the end, don't really want to change anything. They have an initial willing spirit which quickly gives way when they are asked to admit to themselves how their parenting style is contributing to their child's problems. These parents often have poor self-esteem and can't tolerate the most well-intended, constructive, and compassionate criticism.

Any psychotherapist who is knowledgeable about families and children knows that successful treatment of a child's problems almost always includes family treatment of some kind. No child functions in a vacuum. I can work with a child in therapy but if I send them home to the same old environment, whatever progress that child has made will be affected by what is going on in their home. The environment will either support or challenge the changes they are making.

Family dynamics are extremely complicated and people have reasons for behaving the way they do. A family unit fits together psychologically in specific ways, with people playing different roles in order to maintain a certain balance within the family. If one person changes – even if it's one of the children – the rest of the family 'system' has to make changes to accommodate them. If the family is unwilling to do so, there is unconscious pressure on the child to go back to their old ways.

To put it more simply, if I successfully treat a child without their parents being willing to participate actively in their therapy, I may see an improvement rate of anywhere from 20 to 50 percent. If I treat the family, I see improvements more along the lines of 80 or 90 percent. These kinds of outcomes caused me to decide many years ago that I wouldn't accept any children into treatment whose parents weren't willing to actively be involved in the therapy. I tell parents this during the first phone call so that my expectations are clear. I am always relieved when I hear a mother or father respond positively, saying, "We know we need to make changes too" or "We want to be part of the treatment because we know our child isn't having this problem all by themselves."

I want to clarify here what I mean when I refer to 'family treatment'. You may be surprised to know I often end up only treating the parents and never even meeting the child. I recall an instance many years ago in my practice when a teenage girl had a history of so much acting out and defiance that she'd been sent to and expelled from two boarding schools. Her parents felt entirely overwhelmed by her attitude and behavior and sought my help. I met only with the parents for several months, with excellent results. Their daughter's behavior settled down remarkably, solely as the result of changes they made in how they related to her. When I ran into the mother ten years later, she told me her daughter was doing well and never regressed to her former destructive behaviors.

Of course family treatment and parenting changes are not the sole answers for all children. There are children with true psychiatric disorders that need additional kinds of help. These might include schizophrenia or bipolar illness or neurological challenges such as autism, Asperger's Syndrome, or processing, sensory, or attention problems. However, even in these cases, parenting and family changes can be extremely beneficial in helping the child make necessary changes. It is important to perform a thorough evaluation of children who are violent, have significant difficulty relating to others, seem to have attention problems, or suffer any other symptoms that seem severe in nature.

In the following chapters, I will be writing about how our culture has changed over time in ways that are detrimental to children. Parents often feel caught up in the flow of these changes and are lost, seeing the impact of cultural shifts and feeling that current values are wrong but not having any idea what to do about it. Oftentimes, I see parents who want to make changes in how they parent and discipline but do not know if it's right or best for their child.

The relief I see on parents' faces when I talk to them about issues such as respect, autonomy, gratitude, boundaries, and self-control is palpable. It's as if people know what their children need but are afraid to put their foot down and/or follow through with what their instinct tells them to do because they don't see other parents behaving that way. With the support and direction they get in my office, parents often come into their own and start parenting more effectively, often with rapid changes at home.

Do you have the guts to be an independent thinker and not get caught up in a culture that supports entitlement, narcissism, and a lack of self-control when it comes to raising children? Are you willing to do what is best for your children, even if it's different from what other parents are doing? Can you stand up to peer and societal pressure to indulge your children's desire to have everything or to express themselves in whatever way they wish? If so, this book may help you begin to find a way to help your children and help yourself, to find external and internal controls and anchor your family in values and behaviors that feel 'right'. My hope is that some of what I've written might help parents who have lost their way and have no sense of how to stem the tide of narcissism in their children. I will offer concrete direction for effective parenting of children who will grow into responsible, considerate adults. I will refer again and again to the necessity of rising to the occasion to parent your child in the manner they deserve, and what will be required of you to do so.

In my office I can see the reactions of my clients as I impart information. In writing this book, I am offering generalized advice about child rearing and addressing such sensitive topics as discipline and attachment. How each individual interprets what I have written and chooses to apply my recommendations will be up to them.

It troubles me to think any parent would use my ideas to justify harsh treatment of their child or to display a lack of empathic understanding. Exercise good judgment and seek help if you need clarification or support. Take into consideration your child's disposition and inherent strengths and weaknesses when deciding how to approach them.

It is your connection to your child that has the greatest power to influence their behavior. Always view the authoritative aspect of parenting through the lens of loving support. It is by applying both love and discipline that we raise the most well-adjusted children. Although it is not easy, it is essential that we remember our loving attachment to our child, even in the face of acting as their disciplinarians.

There is hope for families and children - and even for our culture – as we move toward a greater sense of responsibility for ourselves and toward each other. In writing this book, it is my goal to help parents become more loving and better able to set realistic expectations for their children. These expectations will in turn help children become more responsible, grateful, and respectful adults. The time for these changes is now.

Narcissism: What is it?

The current tendency to overindulge children without providing them with appropriate expectations for considering the needs of others is the perfect recipe for creating a child who will someday become a narcissistic adult. The term narcissist is commonly used to describe someone who has an overblown sense of their own importance, someone with a 'big ego', or a person who is in love with themselves or their own image. The origins of the term rest in a Greek myth about a young man named Narcissus, who was cursed by the goddess Nemesis and fell in love with his own reflection.

In the field of psychology narcissism has a different and much more pervasive meaning. Narcissistic Personality Disorder is a serious psychological diagnosis with a poor prognosis. The Diagnostic and Statistical Manual of Mental Disorders (DSM) defines this personality disorder as "a pervasive pattern of grandiosity (in fantasy or behavior), need for admiration, and lack of empathy." People with this disorder do poorly in therapy and are rarely motivated to seek such help. There are varying degrees of narcissism as well as varying causes. The most extreme forms are the result of psychological damage early in life and do not diminish with age. There are less severe forms that are exhibited into young adulthood but can decrease with maturity and life experience. In the context of our current culture, this less severe form of narcissism is mostly caused by parents' overindulgence of their children and a lack of appropriate expectations.

What all forms of narcissism have in common is a sense of entitlement, a lack of empathy for others, and inner feelings of emptiness, which one attempts to ameliorate by seeking admiration and attention from others. This inner void is unrelenting; consequently so is the narcissist's bid for recognition. Not having received appropriate reflection from their parents, narcissists constantly look to the current environment for affirmation and mirroring. Whether due to deprivation or overindulgence, the inner void of the narcissist is neverending. What is supposed to 'fill us up' – a sense of self rooted in honesty and a genuine connection with other – simply isn't there.

Narcissists have trouble seeing others as individuals who have their own feelings and needs. Rather, narcissists experience the world through the kaleidoscope of their own inner emptiness and the projection of themselves onto others. This is a concept most people have trouble understanding. If you are not a narcissist, how can you comprehend someone not being able to see you but rather seeing themselves when they look at you? If someone is a narcissist, they almost inevitably are not aware of it and deny it if it is pointed out to them. Narcissists have tremendous difficulty with criticism of any kind, as their self- esteem is poor. They also have a greatly compromised ability to be intimate. How can someone be close with another person whom they can't even really see?

Narcissism obviously hurts those who have to deal with the narcissist, but you shouldn't be fooled into thinking the narcissist isn't suffering too. In their obsession with the self, narcissists may appear to be puffed up and self-satisfied. Those around them often perceive a person with abundant self-esteem and confidence. In reality, however, narcissists struggle with self-hate and an underdeveloped ego; they are never truly satisfied with their intimate relationships or accomplishments.

The choices parents make on a daily basis can help or hinder a child from becoming narcissistic. Parents come to me wanting advice about their children but rarely do they realize how they are contributing to their child's demise. They don't seem to recognize that their parenting style can create offspring who are self absorbed and disrespectful. It is the multitude of choices we make every day as parents that I will be exploring in this book. From discipline to play and work to manners, I address what I believe to be appropriate expectations of children.

When I point out to overindulgent parents that they, in fact, are increasing the likelihood that their children will become narcissistic, they always express grave concern. They become more motivated to change whatever is necessary to keep this from happening. Even parents with no understanding of psychology recognize that being a person who feels special yet empty is no way to live.

In focusing on developing a sense of responsibility and an attitude of gratitude in our children, we help to ensure that they will not grow up to be narcissistic. Rather, they can become individuals who have a realistic view of themselves and their place in the world, someone who has the tools for success in their work and relationships. In deciding to become parents it is our responsibility to raise children who can cope with the world and find inner fulfillment. Parents often tell me their child's happiness is their top priority. Sadly, both our cultural and personal notions of how to create a happy child have become misguided.

Temperament

All parent-child relationships have shared characteristics. All parents struggle with their child's needs as well as their own abilities and limitations. Every child is unique, as is every parent, and every one of us enters this world with an inherent temperament. Each person's nature (or character) is influenced by environment and events but to some extent this is unchangeable. When looking at a course of improvement for children or parents, I always take into account what their basic natures are.

As both a mother and a therapist, I am amazed by the variety of character traits I see in my clients and in my own children; from easygoing to high maintenance, rigid to flexible, outgoing to shy, passive to aggressive, and impulsive to rule-bound, we are all a combination of both likable and unlikable traits. When we decide to become parents, we are making a commitment to accept, nurture, and help our child, no matter who they turn out to be. This is the definition of unconditional love – the kind of love that should be the basis of any parent's feelings for their child.

Children do not ask to be born and parents don't get to pre-order their children's temperaments. How well I remember my experience shortly before the birth of each of my two children. I often sat in the rocking chair in their empty nursery, rocking and wondering who I was about to meet. I was very excited at the thought of my baby finally arriving, even though I had no idea what they would be like. It was a time of wonder and anxious anticipation.

The best kind of parenting takes into account a child's temperament. Sometimes our children's temperaments are very challenging. There are children who are colicky, children who are strong willed, children who are exceptionally bright, children who are slow at learning, children with worrisome natures, and children who are extremely shy or reserved – none of these children have a choice about inheriting these traits. Because we choose to bring them into the world it is our job to do what it takes to parent them effectively.

Why does one mother get to have a placid, happy, and easy-to-put-to-sleep baby while another has one who cries all the time, can't sleep, and is difficult to soothe? This is a largely unanswerable question. The question that does need to be answered is: "How do we cope with these tendencies?" It's okay to feel angry, jealous, or frustrated when it comes to these issues. What is not okay is throwing in the towel and feeling it's more than you can handle.

A colicky baby needs extra patience and soothing. A shy child needs coaching and encouragement. A strong-willed adolescent needs parents who will work together as a team and hold firm to boundaries that will be challenged often. In each of these instances the children deserve to have parents who rise to the occasion of parenting them as is required. That's what the commitment of being a good parent is all about.

Parents and children are not always well matched in their temperaments. In my practice I have encountered parents who are by nature quiet, gentle, and somewhat passive, struggling to raise extremely strong-willed children. I have met aggressive Type-A personality parents who overwhelm their introverted, creative kids. As individuals, one parent may be laissez faire about discipline while the other is demanding and impatient. In all of these instances it is essential for parents to work together and find ways to adapt to their children's natures and for mothers and fathers to come to an agreed-upon course of parenting.

'Difficult' Children

Many books have been written about how to raise a so-called 'difficult' child. Why is it that in today's world the incidence of 'difficult children' is so much higher than it was when I was a kid, in the 1950s and 1960s? Again and again I hear parents say that if they so much as attempted to behave like their own children behave their parents never would have stood for it. Why do parents stand for it now?

A phrase I often use with parents is, "***You have to rise to the same level as your child.***" I use this phrase in reference to a parent matching a child's will and determination. If you are an easygoing person with a defiant or challenging child, you need to build your strength of will so you can discipline them effectively. That means that when you'd rather give in, be easy, or not follow through with an important consequence, you don't.

A child with a strong will needs a parent with enough authority and commitment to help them learn about consequences and self-control. If you give in because you're just too tired or because you feel guilty (thinking, "Other kids get to play on their computer for six hours a day. Maybe I'm being too strict..." or "I've been at work all day and don't want to be fighting with my kid during the little time we have together..."), you are doing your child a disservice.

Children have to learn about self control, self discipline, and the true nature of the world and it is their parents' job to teach them these lessons. If you chronically give in to a strong-willed child or spoil your child by always caving in to their requests, you are creating an individual who won't know how to cope with adult life. The likelihood is high that they will be narcissistic, expecting others to revolve around them while being limited in their ability to think about the feelings or needs of others.

Frustration tolerance is an essential aspect of personality development. How do we cope when we can't or don't get our way?

It forces us to think about things from another person's perspective and/or to reexamine our own wants. If the world doesn't give us what we want, we have no choice but to stop and think about why that is. We all want things we can't have. Learning to cope with that reality and developing a plan for how to better ourselves or change our course of action or thought is one of the basic building blocks of good self esteem and success in all aspects of life.

Giving in to our children's selfish or unrealistic demands promotes a lack of gratitude and respect. So what's the bottom line? No matter how powerful you perceive your child to be, you have to be the ultimate power figure(s) in your family. Get the support you need from others to help you build this strength. Hold yourself in higher regard and expect your children to do the same. Develop a will to parent your child that is as strong as your child's will – and stronger than their demands. Whether your child's temperament is shy or overpowering, cooperative or defiant, it is up you to rise to the challenge of meeting their parenting needs. It takes energy, persistence, and devotion.

In the next chapter we will begin to look at some specific childhood needs and how they can be met with an attitude of mutual respect and love.

Attachment

In this chapter, we will look at your child's most basic need: developing a secure attachment to you, their primary caregivers. Much research has been done to investigate and evaluate different styles of the natural attachment between mothers (usually the primary caregiver) and babies. The lifelong effects of this early attachment are astounding. Research shows that a baby's style of attachment to their parents will overwhelmingly determine what their adult intimate relationships will be like.

The pattern for intimacy – what to expect, how to respond, and how secure we feel – gets hardwired into the brain at a very early age. The good news is that although attachment styles affect virtually every area of intimacy, they can change across time and there is no age limit to when these changes can be made. In adulthood this kind of healing most often occurs through a relationship with a competent therapist. In children it is possible to change how securely attached they feel to their parents even beyond adolescence. That attachment, in turn, can affect their future intimate relationships. For parents it is never too late to work on improving how connected you feel to your child, and vice versa.

Attachment in Infancy

It is your intuitive, emotional connection with your baby that forms the basis for all successful parenting. Psychological literature suggests that the experience of a child being securely attached is described as the child 'feeling felt' by the parent. Tuning in to your baby's affective states, reflecting back to them, and being aware of and respecting your baby's boundaries – particularly when they have had enough contact and want a slight distance – is all part of developing a secure attachment.

It is our job as parents to learn about and tune in to our baby's needs. Sometimes babies desire and need more of us than we feel we have to give. In this regard it is our own sense of responsibility for and respect toward our child that must guide how we parent. Sometimes parents want more interaction with a baby than the baby desires and, as a result, disregard the baby's cues for some distance. Some babies are shy or easily overwhelmed by stimuli. In all of these instances it is the parents' job to work at understanding their child's needs by paying attention to the baby's expressions, body language, and responses.

One aspect of rearing infants that is especially dear to me is the debate over how much a baby should be held. Old-fashioned theories purport that picking up a baby when it cries will 'spoil' the child. Back in the 1960s, it was commonly recommended that parents let a baby 'cry it out' instead of picking them up. I have met and spoken with mothers from that era that followed their pediatricians' recommendation not to pick up their babies, no matter how young the infants were or how much they cried. One of these women described to me the anguish she felt as everything within her told her the doctor's orders were wrong, but she followed them anyway. Thirty years later she still had deep regrets because she hadn't allowed her own instincts to guide her.

How does a parent know when to pick up the baby and when to let the infant cry? Does indulgence of a child's needs start in infancy? The answer to this question is an unequivocal "No". Infants are not born with the ability to self-soothe and their brains are not developed enough to master self-comforting. A baby under the age of six months is completely dependent on the outer world for soothing, and it is through this comfort that the child learns to self-soothe. The baby internalizes the behavior of the parent and learns how to calm themselves down. How can a child learn to self-soothe if it hasn't been soothed in the earliest part of its life?

Self-soothing is another essential criterion for managing adult life. When adults enter therapy and have to confront unresolved issues and emotions, the ability to calm one's self allows for the management of difficult feelings. Without this ability, people can feel flooded and profoundly overwhelmed by their emotional states, often unable to tolerate their feelings or heal them. Soothing your infant in the earliest months of their life can build the foundation of self-mastery, confidence, and the strength to confront difficult situations and emotions.

Soothing your crying baby, taking pleasure in being close to them, allowing yourself to enjoy your bond with your baby through holding and rocking, carrying and cuddling all contribute to the development of a secure attachment with you. In turn, this attachment will allow them to become adults who feel secure in their attachments to their life partners.

Attachment in Toddlers

As our children enter their toddler years, our relationships with them become more complicated. Prior to this the focus of our parenting has been on nurturing, support, and soothing. Now different elements enter our relationship: defiance, power, and control, to name a few. These are just the beginning of challenges parents will have to face for many years to come.

How do we retain a feeling of closeness with a child who has temper tantrums, is uncooperative or no longer wants the kind or amount of cuddling we used to enjoy with them? What if you have a child who is particularly demanding or unreasonable, who embarrasses you in public with their bad behavior or who says hurtful things to you?

The bottom line is that our child's need to feel solidly attached to us does not change at this time even though it may seem otherwise. Toddlers struggle with their need to separate and individuate. Their 'terrible twos' (which often begin around age eighteen months, peak by two and a half, and start smoothing out as they approach three) can feel depressing and overwhelming to many parents. This is a time when some parents begin giving in to their child's demands, believing it is better for the child to be happy in the moment than to be frustrated within themselves or angry with us.

Caving in to your toddler's tantrums is not done out of love. Indulgence and attachment are very different behaviors. Toddlers need to learn how to control their tempers, treat others with respect, and delay gratification. Even if you have worked an entire day and only have one or two hours of time to enjoy with your two-year-old, indulging tantrums is a bad idea. The attachment needs of a toddler are such that they need to know they can rely on you to be there for them, parenting them no matter how they behave. They are at a stage where they will test the parameters of the relationship and it is your job to lovingly, yet firmly live up to what is required of you.

It is your job to teach your child civilized behavior and self-control. I often tell parents in my practice, "The more out of control your child is behaving, the more they are begging you to enforce parental control." Discipline and attachment are not diametrically opposed: Children feel more loved and more securely attached when they have parents who are willing to put the energy into loving, yet firm discipline.

Attachment in Later Years

Parents can sometimes be fooled by their children's behaviors as they mature and move out into the world of peers and social strata. As children grow away from their parents in necessary ways, learning to make connections with others, growing more independent and eventually finding a partner and leaving parents behind as their primary attachment, they often behave as if their attachment to their parents isn't a priority for them. Children will become increasingly embarrassed being seen with their parents in public or amongst their peers.

As children move toward adolescence, these kinds of behaviors intensify. Adolescents engage their parents in power struggles, act defiant, and frequently behave in a rejecting manner. The harsh reality is our kids may seem to want very little to do with us at this point. The purpose of this behavior is the same as it was with our two-year- olds, only now it becomes more sophisticated and often more difficult to handle. Again our children are separating from us. This is a necessary and natural process that will enable them to move out into the world and leave us behind.

In spite of all of these conflicts and behaviors our children's attachment to us remains of the utmost importance. They may be acting as if they could care less what we think of what they do, or as if they wish we'd fall off the face of the Earth, but the reality is that on a deep emotional level our kids still look to us for the limits and engagement they so desperately need. They remain largely emotionally insecure and undeveloped. Our opinions of them matter a great deal.

How can a child take guidance from a parent they can't respect? This often becomes the dilemma for kids of parents who refuse to parent them effectively. Sometimes it is easier to look at systems outside of the family to see more clearly the role that emotional investment and discipline play in the lives of our kids.

One place to observe the positive effects of appropriate authority is in school.

It is often the case that the most involved, strict, yet loving teacher is the most beloved member of the faculty. I have witnessed this in my own children's lives again and again. I can even recall teachers I had in my own junior high school who had high standards, drove us hard, and were held in the highest regard.

An outstanding example of this kind of engagement on all levels is a former choir teacher from a high school in the town where I live. He had extremely high expectations of his students. No tardiness or lack of seriousness about singing was tolerated. He drove them hard to learn complexities about musical theory, made students stand for an entire class period if they were one minute late, and pushed them to learn and perform to the maximum of their abilities and potential.

When that high school closed down, it was difficult to count the number of honors the teacher received, the number of kids who told him he'd changed their lives and the number of alumni who came back to our home town just to acknowledge what he had done for them. Why was this teacher so loved and admired? He had an intense emotional attachment to his students because he devoted endless hours and energy to their growth. This was combined with very high standards for respect and behavior. As a result his students adored him and did exceptionally well.

How many movies are there with such a tale to tell of a teacher who has changed the lives of their students not by giving in to their every whim, but by exacting appropriate authority in the classroom? The loving, yet strict authority figure enters children's lives and as a result the kids learn self-control, self-discipline and achieve better lives and greater happiness.

When parents consult with me about their out-of-control kids, I always emphasize the need for love and affection combined with strict boundaries and consequences. I often tell parents that at the same time they need to sit their kids down and inform them that old rules will be changing, they must also treat their child with increased affection and tenderness when things are going well.

Love and discipline are equally important in raising children. There have been many studies of the long-term outcome of various parenting styles. Three styles of parenting were compared:

Autocratic: These are parents whose main emphasis is on behavior, discipline and control. Attachment is not treated as a priority.

Permissive: These parents show little authority with their children, having minimal boundaries and indulging their children's wishes.

Combination of Autocratic and Loving: In these parent-child relationships, affection and attachment are valued as much as parental control and discipline.

It is probably no surprise to you that the most well adjusted children come from the third group, from parents who are firm, yet loving. However you may be surprised to know how the other two groups fared: The children of autocratic parents were more well adjusted than the children from permissive homes. This shows how essential firm parenting, boundaries and consequences are for a child's normal development.

No matter how much you adore your child and how much you give to them motivated by love, if it isn't paired with appropriate parenting, your child will suffer. Attachment is not a replacement for discipline. It is your job as a parent to react firmly and appropriately when your child is out of line and to show them kindness and affection when things are going well. Some people have trouble moving from one state of mind to another, from frustration and authoritative behavior to tenderness and love. Some parents struggle with ill tempers or a tendency to hold grudges. Other parents feel so worn out they'd rather not engage in a power struggle and simply allow bad behaviors while trying to focus on being close.

Once again let me emphasize, *it is your job as a parent to rise to the occasion – to give your child what they truly need, even if it is hard for you.* Remember that this includes affection as well as discipline. Some parents are not affectionate by nature or don't believe in giving children compliments. I have heard clients say, "My parent believed that as long as they weren't saying something negative, things were okay. They never told me anything good." Others have painfully admitted, "My parents never showed any sign of physical affection or never expressed feelings of love toward me."

Lack of tenderness and affection is damaging to children, and I believe this is the case throughout a child's life. No one is ever too old to enjoy their parents showing them pride, appreciation or adoration. However, children need to know to a certain degree that these feelings must be earned; they are not entitled to adoration, no matter how they behave or what they say.

Attachment in Adulthood

Childhood is the only time in life when we are supposed to receive unconditional love. Clients often tell me they believe marrying someone means there will be an inherent exchange of unconditional love, but that is a myth. Adult attachments are not unconditional. Successful adult relationships are based on accountability and commitment.

When a couple takes their wedding vows, "for richer and poorer, in sickness and in health, in good times and in bad," they are committing to behaving in a loving way toward one another. That does not translate into "I can say and do whatever I want because now that we're married, you have to accept me!"

Self-indulgent behavior in childhood is directly related to self-indulgent behavior in marriage. When children act out and their parents correct them, expecting better of them, children learn an important life lesson: Love equals treating another with respect.

When children are treated like they deserve indulgence, affection and praise no matter how they behave, they aren't able to learn the natural consequences of behaving badly. They don't develop internal controls and sufficient respect for others, both of which are absolute necessities for successful adult attachments. Perhaps when a child is five years old and throwing a screaming fit their parents will tolerate it, but when that same person becomes thirty-five and treats their partner as they did their parents – expecting and demanding immediate gratification, being unwilling or unable to negotiate, and thinking of themselves as the center of the universe – they will suffer miserable relationships and likely be unable to sustain them.

Perhaps half of my practice is made up of couples seeking help with significant marital problems. Increasingly I find myself having to teach younger couples many of the basics of what constitutes a healthy marriage. Many of these couples have the misguided notion that one should freely express what they feel to their partner, no matter the content or tone. The idea of respect as fundamental to a successful relationship seems to have escaped them.

Another common problem in marriage is young adults' inability to negotiate with one another. A lovely, educated young couple came to see me because the wife was bored with the husband after only one year of marriage and was indulging in fantasies about another man at work. When they entered marital therapy, it quickly became evident that although loving, both of these individuals were very immature when it came to understanding what a healthy relationship should look like. She liked to feel unfettered and resented his desire to hear from her during the day or to know when she'd be home. He would indulge in long periods of time playing videogames or insisting they spend most of their weekends with his family. They both tended to lash out at each other when angry. As a result of these difficulties, they had become very alienated from one another and were considering divorce. The husband had retreated into himself, taking a passive stance.

In therapy, I asked this couple to focus on how to act in a more respectful, considerate manner. I told them that screaming at one another was destructive and not all negative feelings need to be expressed. I explained how in adult relationships, each person is accountable for their own behavior, even when it's in response to the behavior of the other. In other words, if I come home from work and my husband or children are irritable or attacking, I don't have license to lash back at them. One person's bad behavior is not license for another's when it comes to marriage or parenthood.

The husband and wife in treatment began listening to the other's requests and considering their merit (empathy) rather than responding with knee-jerk defiance (immaturity and defensiveness). She began calling him from work, and he stopped playing so many video games. They began to balance time alone together with time spent with family and friends. He began to speak up for himself, and she began to listen. The end result was a renewed interest and contentment with the relationship.

All of these traits and skills (empathy, the ability to compromise, control of one's temper and setting priorities that take others into account) are learned in early years through our attachments with our parents. If they are not learned, we will struggle to develop these in adulthood.

Unfortunately the number of people who understand that maturity is essential to a successful marriage seems to be diminishing. Respect seems to be playing a smaller and smaller role in our world in general. It's time for us all to rethink what constitutes emotional freedom and happiness. Respect, gratitude and self control need to be reintroduced to our national mentality and taught as essential elements for successful relationships. If we want our children to have successful intimate relationships as adults, we must begin preparing them from infancy. By giving them unconditional acceptance and affection as infants, discipline and attention in childhood, and limits and love in their teen years, we set the stage for successful partnerships in their future. It is our job as parents to provide all of this to our children. No amount of gifts or privileges, money or opportunities substitutes for our engaged, loving relationships with our kids.

Discipline

In general, our society suffers from a lack of discipline. Employers in today's world have trouble finding young workers who will show up reliably and on time and perform the full extent of their job duties. How many times has a young person waiting on you given you their full attention, acting as if customer satisfaction was a priority? Or were they more interested in texting or talking on their cell phone?

Self discipline and respect for authority figures develops early in life and is a direct result of appropriate parental discipline. The ability to discipline your child when needed is as important for a child's healthy development as showing them love and affection. Unfortunately, many parents are confused about what constitutes discipline in the twenty-first century.

Abuse

The manner in which children are disciplined has changed dramatically in the last fifty years. Much has been learned about the damaging effects of corporal punishment and humiliation. A generation ago, it was commonplace for parents to hit their children as a form of punishment. Physical abuse is no longer considered an acceptable form of discipline, as it's damaging and long- lasting effects have become understood.

In my work with Baby Boomers (adults born during the 1940s and 1950s), I have heard too many accounts of parents using violence to control their children. As a member of that generation, I was also witness to much of this kind of behavior. 'Abuse' was a word no one used at that time.

In my neighborhood and extended family, I saw parents explode at, beat, and even torture their children. This behavior was done in front of others without conscience. No one I knew had even heard of Child Protective Services, let alone made a report to them. The general mentality was that a parent had a right to raise their children however they chose. If a child was born into a violent family, it was their cross to bear, their bad luck.

In my work with clients who have a history of abuse, I have discovered that they inevitably discount, minimize, and even deny the abuse itself and its effects. One client in her fifties told me her mother made her cut a switch off a tree, used to whip her bare skin. Others have told me of severe beatings, hair pulling, being locked into closets or crawl spaces, extreme verbal abuse, constant humiliation, and too many other examples for me to recount. It is not unusual for a client to tell me a detailed story recounting abuse, only to return the following week and announce, "Maybe I'm exaggerating. Maybe it wasn't as bad as I said it was." It is even common for a client to question the reality of what they have told me, saying, "Maybe I'm making it up."

I recall one instance when a client's story of abuse was corroborated by her parent, the abuser, in my office. Later in her therapy, this client voiced denial, questioning if she had fabricated the entire recollection while realizing there was no doubt to the veracity of her story. Such is the profound need for the human mind to protect itself from the reality of the effects of abuse.

Physical and verbal abuse of children is traumatizing. The definition of trauma is "an experience that threatens to overwhelm the brain with anxiety." We are not wired for abuse, and our brains do not have an inherent mechanism for dealing with it constructively in the here and now. When a parent strikes out in anger, it is overwhelming to the child on one level or another. An abused person's only healthy response is *dissociation*, a psychological defense that involves creating distance from the experience by forgetting it, making it unreal, making ourselves unreal, or becoming confused about who we are.

Dissociation is a normal response to trauma, but discipline in childhood should not be traumatic. The reason one tends to minimize the abuse they suffered as a child is because it is just too painful and disturbing to accept.

When one is abused, an internal monitor is created. It is this monitor's job to scan the environment at all times for threats of abuse. This is a survival mechanism that operates on an unconscious level in the form of something called *hyper vigilance*. Hyper vigilance creates a lack of trust, and fear of abuse gets projected into current relationships.

An additional consequence of hyper vigilance is a compromised immune system. When survivors of abuse are successful in therapy, they may thrive in many areas of their lives. However, the part of the brain that scans for ongoing threats is a deeply unconscious and self- protecting mechanism that cannot be fully undone. It takes energy to always be on the lookout for danger. This energy is taken from the mind and body with a resulting compromise in the immune system. It is not unusual for survivors of childhood trauma and abuse to suffer from immune-related chronic illnesses.

The effects of physical and verbal abuse of children are far reaching. Shame, trouble modulating anger, self hate, self destructive behaviors, lack of trust, and poor self esteem are just a few of the remnants therapists deal with in clients who have a history of abuse.

If I grow up with a parent who explodes and swears at me whenever they are the least bit frustrated, I will tend to either copy this behavior in my adult relationships or fear being a victim of it. As a result, intimacy becomes more of a challenge. Depression and withdrawal are common in those with a history of abuse.

Because we have learned the price children – and society consequently – pays for abuse, parents have been taught not to mistreat their children. Most parents are no longer comfortable with the notion that their children are theirs to do with as they wish. Fortunately, we have learned that abuse is not an acceptable form of punishment.

As abuse has become socially unacceptable, many parents have become confused about the role discipline plays in raising children. If a parent can't lash out in frustration and hit as a way of instilling fear and respect, what are they to do? If it's not alright to terrorize one's child, is it acceptable to instill fear through the exercise of authority? Many people are confused about what respect for a parent's authority should look like.

Authority vs. Abuse

When someone has authority over us, whether it's a teacher, a boss, or a government official, there is the potential for us to feel afraid of that person. By virtue of their position, they hold certain amount of power over us. If I am driving down the street observing the speed limit and see a police car in my rear view mirror, I don' t need to feel afraid because I'm not doing anything wrong. If I'm going ten miles over the speed limit, I will be fearful that I could be pulled over and given a speeding ticket. Why would I be fearful in such a situation? It is because I know the officer holds the power to inflict an unwanted consequence on me. It is that fear that forces me to monitor my driving habits.

It is hard to imagine where parents ever got the idea that their children should not see them as powerful authority figures. We have tremendous power over our children, whether we choose to think of ourselves that way or not. Their lives rest in our hands for many years. We have the power to make them feel good or terrible about themselves. We can create a nurturing, supportive environment or a negligent and devastating one.

Young children view their parents as all-powerful and depend on that perception to help them feel secure. The parent is viewed as an omnipotent being that can ward off all danger and conquer any threat. Children need to believe we can save them from everything because they feel so vulnerable in the world.

Becoming a parent is an awesome responsibility. Exercising our power, authority, and discipline over a child is part of that responsibility. Parents must always be in control of themselves when handing out discipline. Our power must be used wisely and with compassion. Just as our children need to believe we can protect them from all harm, they need to rely on us to teach those limits, self restraint, and respect. They need to rest in the assurance that we will exercise our authority as needed in order to help them learn how to manage in the world. This is part of a parent's commitment to their child.

In our own exercise of discipline, we must have self control, restraint, and respect for our child. This model will be internalized and further teach our children how to responsibly manage frustration.

Being Your Child's Friend

Increasingly, I see parents in my office who desire to shirk authority over their kids in exchange for the kind of intimacy that exists between friends. These mothers and fathers want their children to feel safe with them, loved, and accepted at all times. Parents' increased involvement in their children's lives has led many to think of themselves as peers rather than authority figures.

Some mothers and fathers have a need to feel close to their child at all times and have difficulty tolerating any conflict, no matter how temporary. "I want my child to like me" is a statement I frequently hear when the topic of discipline comes up.

My answer to these parents is: "Your children do not need you to be their friend. They need you to be their loving and helpful parent." Sometimes being a parent means being close, playful, and having fun. At other times, however, it means being an authority figure that can hand out and follow through with discipline. *If you are getting your own needs for closeness met through your relationship with your child while sacrificing their needs for parenting and discipline, you are failing your child.*

In order to discipline appropriately, you have to be willing to tolerate the discord and distance that is temporarily created in your relationship with them. There is a momentary 'rupture' in our attachment with our child. Remember that this is normal and not harmful, as long as it is followed by a 'repair' to that attachment in short order. The repair is a result of behaviors on both the child's and the parents' parts. If the child has done something wrong, they need to apologize, take responsibility, and reach out. The parent needs to teach, forgive, and reach back. These kinds of interactions teach your child accountability, remorse, empathy, and communition – all valuable and necessary attributes for their adult relationships.

Think of all that children are missing out on when their parents won't take the time or effort to discipline them! This is very frustrating for me. Parents who allow their kids to run wild are simply not doing their job and are failing to recognize that others are offended by their child's behavior, as if they are functioning in a vacuum. The wild child doesn't learn that their behavior has a social context. Because the parents are out of touch with social mores and how others perceive or are being bothered by their children, the child doesn't learn to see himself as part of a social group. Instead, the child learns they don't have to consider the feelings or opinions of others. They become entitled and cut off from an important feedback loop.

We need to act like the authority figures our children need us to be. Children are not born as civilized beings. They have to be taught basic social behavior and control of bodily functions, and they look to us as authorities to help them along the way. Who will they learn appropriate behaviors from if not from us? How can we exert any authority over them if our main concern is being a friend rather than a parent to them?

You can't be a competent parent if your main goal is to be your child's friend. As a society, we need to face the reality that children need to be parented, not befriended by the adults who are responsible for them.

Most parents who come to see me don't like the idea of their children being intimidated by them. Some of them have their own memories of being terrorized and abused by a parent. Again, it is important to recognize the difference between being abused and being authoritatively parented. Acting like an authority figure does not entail cruelty, explosiveness, or humiliation. Our power should be expressed in a mature, self controlled and caring way.

Appropriate authoritative parenting does not preclude play and closeness with our children; it's simply that these pleasurable activities do not replace a child's need for direction, regulation, and the development of self restraint. A loving bond with our child that includes affection, fun, and admiration feeds their respect for us. In turn, this enhances their desire to please us and be more receptive to discipline. Attachment and discipline go hand in hand when it comes to creating a sense of security in a child.

Disciplining as a Team

In two-parent families, it is essential for parents to have an agreed-upon set of rules for children and to share in the enforcement of consequences. This is easy to say but often not so easy to implement. Each of us has our own nature to contend with. It is common for parents to inherently respond to conflict differently, even within our own families. To further complicate matters, parents are vulnerable to acting out their own conflicts with their children. Sometimes parents are aware of what they're doing, and sometimes they aren't.

It's not unusual for me to see a mother or father in my private practice who tells me they are intentionally parenting their child very differently from how they were raised. For instance, if they had parents who refused to help them when they struggled with school, they go out of their way to be sure they are a help to their child in this area.

Compensating for one's childhood with one's own children can be a good thing, but sometimes parents go too far and end up overindulging their child. This type of overindulgence seems to be something parents have an awareness of and are often able to identify in their therapy with me. It's common for me to hear a mother or father say, "My parents were so hard on me that I went to the other extreme and haven't been strict enough with my kids." This is usually said in an undefended manner, and the parents who say it are often open to changing their behaviors.

Unfortunately, this is not what occurs in most of families I work with. When parents consult me regarding a child who is having behavioral problems, the overwhelming majority of the time, the parents can't agree with each other about what to expect from their child or how to enforce consequences. Sometimes parents play good cop/bad cop, and one parent is the disciplinarian while the other gets to remain buddies with the child.

In most of the families I work with, I hear one parent complain that the other is too passive about discipline and consequences. The parents frequently fight with each other about what to do with their unruly child. Typically, one parent is overly responsive to their kid's acting out while the other does little. There is usually a great deal of conflict and resentment between parents surrounding this issue. Frequently, the more passive parent dislikes the stricter parent's approach and withdraws so as not to participate in the exchange. This is a dysfunctional response, as it leaves the child alone with an angry parent and leaves the angry parent alone with no one to help manage the child.

I typically see tremendous relief in the disciplining parent when I encourage a passive parent to step up and help their partner set limits. In some families, the mother or father has been fighting for this kind of help for a long time but has given up.

Just this week, I saw a sixty-year-old woman who had struggled with this issue with her daughter and husband for many years. At age thirty-three, the daughter had a long-term history of spoiled, irresponsible behavior and nastiness toward the mother. The father refused to say or do anything about it. This woman had walked out on her family during an argument over the daughter being negligent of her own children. In response to her husband's unwillingness to become involved in the discussion in any way, this client had left her home and was staying with her other adult daughter and talking of separation and divorce. She was in crisis; her husband's passivity had become unbearable to her.

It is unwise to put the onus of being the strict parent on one person. Although by nature one parent may be 'tougher' than the other, families and children do best when parents share the responsibility of discipline. Having a shared and consistent message of expectations affords children a clear understanding of how to behave and what consequences will be involved if they do not. There is less confusion and less conflict between family members. There is also less opportunity for children to manipulate parents against one another. When a second parent steps in to reinforce what the first parent is saying, the message carries more weight, and the child sees a united front. The decrease in confusion and increase in clarity helps kids calm down, feel more secure, and have a better sense of direction. Making this singular change of co-parenting can alter the course of a child's misbehavior in a dramatic way.

The following is a case where two parents' differing responses to their child's misbehavior had serious consequences:

Twelve-year-old Julia was brought to me by her parents after failed treatment with two other therapists. Julia's behavior at school was fine, but she was a tyrant at home. She had free-wheeling rages and showed little inhibition in how she expressed anger. Julia often hit her mother, called her terrible names, and refused to cooperate. This had been going on for several years, and by the time the family got to me, the mother was burned out and even somewhat numb in response to her daughter's aggression. I witnessed Julia physically lashing out at her mother in my waiting room with no repercussions. When I confronted the mother about this, she stated she hadn't even felt her daughter hit her. There was such a long history of this kind of behavior that the mother had become dissociated in response to her daughter's abuse.

What I discovered when I had the parents come in to meet alone with me was somewhat shocking. The father described how he admired his daughter's feisty spirit, even smiling when he talked about her out-of-control behaviors. He stated that he found her 'funny' and chose not to discipline her in any way. I explained to this man how what he found 'funny', others found alarming and frightening, and how his lack of parenting was setting his daughter up to become an unsocialized and miserable adult. This information surprised and upset him.

In reality, this man's acceptance of his child's outrageous behaviors was driven by a vicarious pleasure he took in her expression of anger. He was a quiet and passive man with a childhood history of abuse at the hands of an angry father. His daughter was acting out the kind of anger he himself wanted to express. This vicarious gratification was so great that it blinded him to the reality of his daughter's troubled behaviors.

In response to treatment, the father began speaking up and disciplining his daughter, acting as a united front with his wife. Their child's behavior immediately improved and continued to do so over time. He required occasional sessions to keep him on track and encourage his newfound style of parenting. Julia made significant improvements but ultimately left therapy prematurely. The many years of acting out that her parents had tolerated had taken a terrible toll on her and made it difficult for her to progress beyond a certain point in the treatment. She had not developed the internalized sense of control she needed to make increasingly difficult changes in her behavior. She had succeeded only partially in therapy and left on a bad note, after locking herself in the bathroom in response to a discussion about expecting more of herself in a certain regard. Julia's self confidence had been devastated by her own acting out over time. Sadly, she was unwilling to return to treatment after having successfully improved her attitude and behaviors by perhaps 60 percent.

Cultural Shift

In addition to how parents have been affected by their personal histories, cultural shifts have also contributed to confusion about authority and discipline. Much has changed in the last fifty years regarding cultural notions about individual expression and personal freedom. Some of these ideas have bled into areas of parenting that should have been left alone. Let's take a look at how the mentality of a social and political movement infiltrated the styles of parenting.

During the sixties and early seventies, there was a rebellion against authority and autocratic thinking in America. Freedom of expression and individuality became prized as young people rose up against the leaders of the day. The 'younger generation' developed distaste for values held by the World War II generation. Conformity, duty, and preconceived notions of right and wrong were suddenly being questioned and defied. The thinking of the day was: "I am me, and you are you. I am not here to make you happy, but to be myself."

The idea that teenagers or young adults should act a certain way because older adults 'said so' underwent scrutiny and upheaval. Previously held ideas and rules were open to new interpretations. The result? Dramatic changes in our society, some of great value. Women's rights, racial equality, and the sexual revolution are a few of the ideas that gained momentum.

Unfortunately, much of what is valuable about authority and discipline also seemed to somehow get lost in the societal and cultural shifts. There are remnants of this cultural shift that affect current-day parenting.

This problem has been growing exponentially in recent years. There seems to be a new cultural norm for children to speak to adults with disrespect, have little self control, and expect some form of stimulation at all times. How many of us have had the experience of watching children behave completely out of control in public places while their parent does nothing? As an observer of these kinds of events, I often feel angry when I see parents failing their children by neglecting their responsibilities to parent them. I wonder, "What will happen to that child when they become an adult? Will they suddenly realize that impulse-driven behavior is unacceptable and develop the appropriate internal controls?"

Making these kinds of changes is very difficult. The older a child is, the harder it is to change their behaviors through external discipline or internal motivations. In adulthood, it is even harder to alter long- held, habitual behaviors, although it can be done.

I believe it is essential for our culture to start moving in a different direction if there's to be any hope for the one that follows. Appropriate respect for authority, self discipline, and self control seem to be falling by the wayside. It amazes me that parents don't seem to realize raising children with a lack of discipline creates unhappy, out-of-control kids.

Let's look at some common problems parents face when it comes to choosing forms of discipline and how to enforce them.

Discipline and Temperament

Deciding on the most effective form of discipline for your child is not always easy. Different temperaments in children require different responses from parents. Anyone who is familiar with child rearing knows that some kids are much easier to discipline than others.

I have two grown children, a son and a daughter. Their natures are very different. Although they share values and several personality traits, disciplining them could not have been more disparate.

My son, the older of the two, was born with an adventurous, strong-willed nature. To say he's a self-determined individual is to put it mildly. Disciplining him was a challenge throughout the course of his entire childhood and adolescence. He was one of those rare children who was never swayed by consequences. No matter what was taken away from him, he would suffer the loss and continue moving along the same path.

My daughter, on the other hand, has always been highly rule bound and sensitive to disapproval by others. Her inner drive to 'do the right thing' is relentless, even when she's been encouraged to loosen up and break a few rules.

My experience dealing with them as toddlers was completely divergent. My son required frequent time-outs and would sometimes refuse to stay where he was supposed to sit. I have vivid and funny/painful memories of putting him in his room at age five, having to hold the door shut while he struggled on the other side to get out because he refused to accept his five minutes of time-out. This is something I felt very conflicted about, and it wasn't my idea of what discipline was supposed to like.

On the other hand, my daughter had only one time-out in her entire childhood. When she was two years old and being openly defiant about something, I sat her in the time out chair in my dining room, and within thirty seconds she began sobbing as if her world was crumbling. I picked her up immediately, we had a talk about it, and I don't think I even had to threaten a time out after that.

Like my daughter, some children are compliant by nature. They want to please their parents and are sensitive to criticism or disapproval. They can be overly tuned in to even small signals from a parent that something is wrong. Generally speaking, this kind of child is easy to discipline. They respond favorably to consequences, and a gentle verbal reprimand is often adequate.

If you have a child who has always been easy to discipline and is bent on pleasing you, adolescence will likely bring new challenges for discipline. As they get older and need to separate and emancipate emotionally, parents may start to see uncooperative or defiant behaviors. This is extremely normal, a sign that your child feels secure enough to separate from you. I will be addressing the issue of adolescents and discipline later in this chapter.

Other children are less concerned about what others think of them and more focused on their own agenda. Although it may seem like they don't care if you get angry with them, internally they are in distress when their parents disapprove. Some children can mask this distress so effectively that their parents can't see it.

In studies done with eighteen-month-old children, it has been proven that although some toddlers show no external signs of discomfort when separated from a parent, their physiology is in a state of upset. Some children learn at an alarmingly early age to hide their anxiety and show no signs of inner turmoil. My advice is for parents to assume their child is always impacted by their responses, even when that doesn't appear to be the case. This applies to subtle cues as well as obvious reactions they display. The basis for all discipline is the belief that our children want to do what is right and to please us, even when it appears entirely otherwise.

A seventeen-year-old girl was brought to see me because of her explosiveness, verbal abuse of her parents and siblings, defiance of her parents' rules, and inability to accept limits. During her first session, the girl broke down into tears. "I'm the bad one in the family," she said. "My brother is the good one. The only way I could be good is if I died and came back as someone else." It was painful to see someone so young feel so completely hopeless about themselves. It's important to note this was not the persona that the girl showed her parents.

Regardless of their child's temperament, I see many parents in my office who have trouble disciplining their children. It's as if the very idea of a well- disciplined child has lost its value. Indulgence and wanting to be 'liked' by one's child seems to have taken the place of parental authority.

Consistency

Parents who seek my help for their out-of-control kids almost always tell me the same story when it comes to discipline. They threaten consequences and frequently talk to their children with appropriate authority. Ninety percent of the time, these same parents tell me they are not good at consistency and often don't follow through with consequences.

Giving your child consequences but not being consistent is like being a diabetic who watches their diet until four o'clock each day and then eats an entire chocolate cake. Consequences and punishments are meaningless if you don't follow through with them.

It is common for parents to lose their tempers in the moment, threatening unrealistic consequences they have no intention of carrying out. "My daughter lied to me about why she was on the computer. I got really mad and told her she couldn't use it for a month." This is usually followed by, "I was just so mad that I ended up saying something I didn't mean. I let her have it back after two days."

What are your children learning when you say things out of anger that you don't mean or enforce? They learn not to trust what you say. They learn you are impulsive and reactive when you're angry. They calculate what you really mean (based on your past behavior) and come to their own conclusions. They lose respect for you. Often, they learn that you can be manipulated into changing your mind. In short, they learn they can't rely on what you say. On a deeper level, this translates into learning they can't rely on you.

It is better to not give your child a consequence at all for their bad behavior than to threaten one and not follow through with it. This is partly because of the role that intermittent reinforcement plays in the human mind. Inconsistent, intermittent reinforcement is extremely powerful. The idea that we can get away with something some of the time excites the brain. The anticipation of whether or not we will 'win' is similar to the anticipatory brain chemistry that gambling addicts deal with. People who gamble don't win most of the time; they only win occasionally. The excitement of this unknown outcome is part of what makes gambling so alluring.

Children love to test their parents. Even the best-behaved child wants to know how reliable their parents are. Testing a parent's limits and resolve are a child's way of finding out how serious the issue at hand is, how serious the parent is about it, and how committed the parent is to follow through.

The more difficult the child or situation, the more important it is for a parent to follow through with consequences. With firm external limits, the child learns to limit their own behaviors and impulses. It is only through consistent responses and consequences that children learn their parents are serious about the limits being set.

Sometimes parents feel 'burned out' when it comes to dealing with challenging situations, and they start getting lazy about following through. A common complaint I hear from my clients is, "My kid is going through a phase where they're driving me crazy. I feel like all I do all day is say 'no' and discipline them. It's depressing." My response? "Some phases of parenting aren't fun. Sometimes we don't get to be the kind of parents we want to be. I'm sure you'd rather have a kid right now that you could cuddle with and be sweet to, but that's not what they need at the moment."

Although parents often look deflated when I say this, I also notice they feel relieved and reassured. Somewhere along the annals of time people, have started believing that being a good parent means being supportive and tolerant all the time. That is nonsense! When your child is going through a troublesome developmental phase, they often aren't fun to be around. They are changing in some way that requires them to create distance from you. It is your job to respond to these challenges consistently, even when it makes your job as a parent unpleasant over a potentially extended period of time.

In some families, it is common for parents to become less consistent and firm with their younger birth order children. Whereas expectations of their older kids were clear and included appropriate consequences, younger children are not held up to the same standards. A modicum of this kind of change is natural as parents learn what they need to control across time. However, I have seen families in which parents have done their younger children a disservice by being too worn out to put in the required effort to set appropriate limits. Consistency needs to exist within the family across all children, and not just with one particular child. There must be rules that apply to all members of the family, parents included.

Consequences

Most children's behavior can be modified through administering consequences. Once again, personality differences need to be taken into account when determining what consequences to give your child.

How do you decide what an appropriate consequence is for your child? One simple solution is to look at your child's life and find something they would miss if they lost it. I am not talking here about attachment objects such as favorite stuffed animals, security blankets, etc. I'm referring to objects or privileges used for fun.

In today's tech-savvy world, it's usually not that hard to find something your child would miss if it were gone. For youngsters, disallowing a favorite TV show, computer or video games, or treats such as special snacks will often work. For older kids, taking away computer time, cell phones, and iPods or setting stricter curfews or grounding is usually effective. Your children won't be harmed by having these luxuries taken away for reasonable periods of time when they misbehave.

For smaller children, time outs can be very effective. Sitting in a time-out chair – or being sent to their room if they are old enough – are a couple of possibilities. The general formula is one minute for each year of age. Set a timer and go to your child when it goes off. At that point, they should apologize and make up with you. Sometimes apologies are insincere. I tell parents to expect a sincere apology and let their child know that is what it will take for them to get out of time out.

Some consequences are difficult to enforce. If you are going to give a consequence, it's your job to make it happen! I hear parents bemoan having to carry computer keyboards in their trunks, get special plugs that can be removed from TVs, having to cope with not being able to contact their children without cell phones, and more.

Your follow through on consequences is absolutely necessary if it is to be effective in the long run. If you tell your child, "No computer for three days!" be prepared to disconnect a keyboard or mouse. If they need to use the computer for schoolwork, they will have to use it only in your presence so you can monitor what they are doing.

I realize that access to technology makes these kinds of consequences a pain to follow through with, but it can and should be done. The outcome justifies all the effort required, and it's worth it for you and for your children in the end.

Consequences for Adolescents

It is normal for adolescents to strike out on their own, defining their own tastes and values and doing some high risk behaviors. Adolescents are notorious for having terrible judgment. This poor judgment allows them to engage in risky behaviors. These behaviors are biologically driven and allow them to create distance from their parents, take chances, and learn their own lessons.

Discipline with adolescents is inherently different than with younger children. When our kids are small, we try to protect them from suffering negative consequences. We do this by teaching, disciplining, and punishing bad behaviors. We create the negative consequences for their poor choices.

Adolescents learn about adult life through their own choices and the natural repercussions of their decisions. A necessary transition in an adolescent's life is increased freedom, which comes with the responsibility of making their own choices and learning from them. The parent has to get out of the way and allow their teen to go through this process. Whereas our role up until that time is proactive, parents of teens now are relegated to the role of observer, advisor, and coach.

This doesn't mean adolescents are never disciplined by their parents. Grounding, loss of privileges, and temporary diminishment of their freedoms are all appropriate. However, it is best whenever possible to step aside and allow your teen to suffer the natural negative consequences of their own behavior and choices.

One of my clients, the forty-eight-year-old mother of a teenage girl, struggled with her daughter's propensity for staying up half the night and being unable to get up for school in the morning. To combat the problem, she found herself rushing her daughter out of bed at the last minute and racing to get her to school on time. Then my client would hurry to her own job as a teacher, missing out on important planning time she needed each morning.

My advice to this frustrated client was to sit down with her daughter and discuss a schedule for the morning and the consequences if her teen couldn't or wouldn't follow through. A departure time was to be set and adhered to, or her daughter would have to find her own way to school. If her daughter couldn't get to school on time and lost credit for a class as a result, she would have to live with that consequence. The end result was a few missed days, followed by her daughter learning to be on time.

Some teens show such poor judgment and motivation that they are willing to suffer fairly extreme consequences without changing their behavior. Even then, parents need to step back and allow the natural end results to prevail. Your adolescent won't learn about consequences if you are there to protect them from them.

In raising my own children, this shift in parenting was the most difficult transition I ever had to make. I had spent twelve or thirteen years keeping a watchful eye on my child and interceding to protect him/her from harm. Once they reached adolescence, other than offering guidance and warnings, I had to learn to step back and let them fall. I had to watch as they made bad decisions, not realizing the future implications of their actions and often getting hurt and feeling bad about themselves in the process.

During that time, I often told my friends it felt like I was standing on a sidewalk, watching my three-year-old run into the street and doing nothing about it. It was very hard for me to convince myself that holding back and letting them learn from self-inflicted pain was more loving and supportive than saving them from the consequences of their own decisions.

This is a frightening but necessary part of raising adolescents. In addition to the consequences we give them for breaking rules such as coming home late, not calling, or lying to us, we have to be strong enough not to intervene to save them from their own poor choices. This is a huge shift in both the role we play as parents and the attribution of responsibility to our kids.

It takes real toughness and love to have faith in our adolescents, especially when they are making bad choices. We must remember that they won't always be as they are today. It's not that our role as teachers ends, but rather that most adolescents have lost a good part of their interest in being our students.

Even when teens appear to be blowing off what we say to them, they do hear us. Often, they internalize what we say, and sometimes it takes years before we see the end results. Not all teens get there.

An exception to stepping back and allowing natural consequences for your teen is when drugs, alcohol, or sexual promiscuity are involved. Too much damage can be done for us to allow poor judgment to prevail. Another time to step in is if your child is showing sudden changes in behavior. Signs of depression, significant changes in sleeping and eating habits, and social withdrawal all need to be addressed.

It can be a delicate balancing act deciding when and how to involve ourselves in our teen's life. Many books have been written on the subject, and there are widely divergent opinions on how to cope with your adolescent. I have attempted here to address the need for natural consequences in your teen's life and the transition in our role from disciplinarian to coach. Don't get in the way of your teen and keep them from learning what they need to from life unless they are at risk while doing so. We all have to struggle to find our way from childhood to adulthood, and very few of us have gotten there with only good choices behind us. Some of us go through very turbulent times in our teens. In my practice, I always encourage the parents of adolescents to talk to other parents of teens for support and feedback. It's just too hard and confusing of a job to do alone.

Don't forget that your teen still very much needs your love, affection, and communication, whether you are the one setting a consequence or watching them cope with the after effects of their own choices. Continue to talk to your adolescent and offer guidance. It is your job to teach what is right, even when it appears that you have an unwilling student in your teen. Love–combined with appropriate expectations and consequences–will help them navigate those difficult years.

In the next chapter, we will look at respect as the basis for all successful relationships from early childhood through old age.

Respect

As a psychotherapist in private practice, I have the opportunity to watch children interacting with parents in my waiting room before and after a session, as well as under more monitored circumstances in my office. I must confess it is disheartening to see the grand scale of disrespect I observe almost daily. From the youngest child to adult children, I frequently see disparaging looks, outright defiance, name calling, insults, and even physical aggression. Sometimes it seems I'm witnessing the very breakdown of society right in my office.

How have we ended up this way? Since when has this become a new cultural norm? Just today, walking home from my office, I saw a father playing with his son on the playground. The boy looked to be about five years old and was 'playfully' hitting his father repeatedly with an angry look on his face. The father did and said nothing about it. Instead, he responded by turning it into play and hitting the boy back in the same manner. It was clear to me this man believed there was nothing wrong with what his son was doing.

Last week, one of my clients was complaining about a friend who allowed her four-year-old daughter to hit her without any consequences. This led to the problem of that child being overly aggressive with my client's young son. My client didn't know what to do about the situation. She feared her friendship with the woman might have to come to an end.

Two weeks ago, parents came in to see me about their teenage daughter, who is prone to tantrums and defiance. They described to me how their daughter had exploded, culminating in her pounding her father with her fists. These parents didn't know how to respond, though this wasn't the first time it had happened.

And these examples are just from the last two weeks!

Other more extreme examples are the seventeen-year-old girl who swore at her parents with abandon, breaking almost all of their rules, frequently lying to them and telling them she had no respect for them; the twelve-year-old boy whose parents sent him to an expensive private school, where the principal had to come out to the parking lot to try to convince this tantrum-prone boy to come into the building; the eleven-year-old girl who swore at, demeaned, and hit her mother right in my office and waiting room; the fifteen-year-old girl who always talked to her mother with impatience and disgust every time they were in my office; and the list could go on and on.

You may think these are unusual or extreme examples, but sadly, they are not. Unfortunately, they are becoming commonplace. I literally have to instruct parents, right in front of their children, not to allow their children to lay their hands on them or speak to them with disrespect.

I have to wonder, do parents not know how wrong these behaviors are? They complain freely about these same kinds of interactions when they're alone with me but seem to be confused and/or helpless to do anything about it when with their kids. Why is that? If they know it's wrong, why aren't they stopping their kids?

I find that many parents are confused about what is best for their children in this regard. They know it feels wrong when their kids are disrespectful, but they look at the culture around them and become uncertain. They compare their children to their peers and see so much of this kind of behavior that they start to question if it's really wrong.

The reason I titled this book *Have the Guts to Do It Right* is because I see too many parents who do not have the courage to follow what their own gut is telling them to do. Deep inside, they feel troubled by what is going on, but they don't trust their own judgment enough to be guided by their internal responses.

Do most people believe children should respect their parents? Yes, they do. Do most of these kinds of kids who come into my office know they are being disrespectful? When I ask them, their answer is almost always "Yes." Most of these children openly admit they are upset by their own behavior and want to be more respectful. They are often surprisingly receptive to my suggestions as to how they can treat their parents better, control their tempers, and stop acting like they are the center of the universe.

But if the parents and the child all know the behavior is unacceptable, why is it happening? When I ask parents why they tolerate disrespect, they say they don't know how to stop it. Frankly, I don't believe this.

It is my experience in working with families that most parents *do* know how to stop bad behavior in their children, but they won't give themselves the permission to take it seriously enough to make it happen. This is where lack of consistency and consequences takes over, along with confusion and passivity.

My advice to parents is to tolerate zero disrespect from their kids. Almost all parents seem very surprised when I say this. So many people have come to believe that disrespect is part of being a child or adolescent and that it's the parents' burden to bear, but this could not be further from the truth.

Disrespect vs. Anger

In previous generations, any expression of anger by a child was oftentimes judged as disrespectful. I grew up in a house where the word "No" wasn't allowed. Even healthy expressions of frustration weren't acceptable. I know my family wasn't unusual in this regard because I saw the same standards in my friends' families. In response to this oppressive stance, the pendulum has swung too far in the opposite direction. Open, blatant disregard and disrespect have somehow become acceptable.

Disrespect and anger is not the same thing. Many parents seem to have trouble making this distinction. They mistakenly believe that when their child is talking to them with a tone of disgust or contempt, they are just expressing anger. Some are even accepting of their child's physical aggression and view it as a simple form of venting frustration.

Healthy expressions of anger are not damaging to your child or their relationship with you. Anger can be very intense without it being destructive or lacking in respect. How can a parent know where the line is between anger and disrespect? My first answer is that your gut will probably tell you. When your child's comments become hurtful, condescending, sarcastic, or nasty, they have crossed the line. It is one thing to say, "It's not fair that I can't go out tonight! You never let me do what I want!" but it is quite another to say, "I hate you! You're stupid!" or "I'm not listening to you!"

Physical aggression should never, ever be tolerated. I would apply this to children of all ages, even the very young. Babies or toddlers sometimes like to bite or hit. They need to be taught very firmly that this is not acceptable. This can be done by looking your child right in the eye while holding onto them and speaking with authority about it. Your tone will let your child know physical violence is a serious matter and won't be tolerated.

Some people believe biting their child back or spanking is a way to teach nonviolence. The irony of this is obvious. You should be able to control your child's behavior without having to resort to hitting and therefore disrespecting them yourself.

When kids reach the point where they are hitting their parents, they have lost control. I would say the same about children whose mouths have run wild. As a parent, you must be the external control that stops the behavior.

Disrespect in Adolescence

Everyone knows how difficult teens can be. They have their own minds and are frequently at odds with any authority figures, parents included. They are fighting for the right to run their own lives and questioning much about our judgment. Their own judgment is impaired by hormonal influences and previously described risk-driven behavior.

This is where I typically see the most out-of-control expressions of disrespect toward parents. Adolescents themselves are very poor judges of social interactions. Studies have shown that teens and adults in their early twenties are unable to identify blatant emotional expressions on a human face. It's not until age twenty-five that this fully changes. This means teenagers are poor judges of how they should be acting with you much of the time. They are emotionally excitable, impulsive, and yearn to test the limits of social relationships.

When angry with their parents, adolescents can 'flex their muscles', getting madder and madder and seeing how intimidating they can be. They will test the limits of their power with you. Now that they are as big as you (or bigger in some cases), they want to know if they can subjugate you. If they fiercely believe they are right and you are wrong, can they disregard what you have to say? Do they still have to treat you with respect, even as they are questioning your knowledge and intelligence?

Although there will likely be more arguments and power struggles as your child moves from their preteen years to adolescence, it doesn't mean there should be any change in the amount of respect they show you. ***The rule of thumb should still be zero tolerance for disrespect.*** Your teen needs to learn how to express anger or disagreement without accompanying sarcasm, vindictiveness, or cruelty.

My general recommendation to parents is to stop a conversation after the first sentence if your teen begins yelling at you.

Simply inform them they are not allowed to yell at you and that it absolutely won't be tolerated. The conversation at hand will only continue when they have calmed down enough to stop yelling. Just as I disagree with hitting a child who is hitting you, I strongly advise against yelling back at your teen. Adolescents are often trying to get us to relate to them at their own level, and they can be experts at provoking us.

When your teen begins to yell or show signs of disrespect, stop them immediately and disengage. Some teens will stop if you make it clear that you refuse to continue until they change their attitude. Others can be very persistent, continuing to yell or even following if you try to walk away. Even when this is the case, parents must find away not to engage. It may even be necessary to go to another room and shut the door if your teen won't respect your need for distance until they change their attitude.

It is also appropriate to administer consequences for disrespectful behavior. One of my clients takes her daughter's cell phone away for two days every time her daughter speaks disrespectfully to her. Although not always necessary, this type of consequence can be very effective for children who don't take warnings seriously.

The bottom line is that teenagers should be treated no differently than younger children when it comes to respecting parents. Disagreements – no matter how passionate or frequent – should be handled in a respectful manner. By nature, teens may be more volatile and emotional but that doesn't mean they have a newfound right to treat you badly.

I tell teens in my practice that angry or hateful thoughts are normal and don't hurt anyone. I explain the difference between having a feeling and expressing it. Interestingly, the teens themselves are often quick to catch on to this concept, but their parents have more trouble. Many parents believe it is healthy for their child to vent anger and frustration in whatever way they wish, but this is a ridiculous and unhealthy assumption. Your teen may think they hate you, but it's not acceptable for them to freely express it. You are the person who supports, raises, and struggles with them. They are not entitled to behave badly because of their inner battles.

Sibling Bickering

Almost every parent that comes into my office eventually complains to me about the amount and intensity of bickering that goes on between their children. Sometimes, this is the primary complaint that will bring a family into treatment. Parents often identify one child as the instigator. It is not uncommon for me to hear a mother or father say, "Our kids fight all day long" or "They argue about everything."

I liken the issue of chronic fighting among siblings to the topic of disrespect because parents seem to believe it's just part and parcel of raising children. Like disrespect, this behavior contributes significantly to creating an unhappy home life for all involved. The constant fighting causes a general sense of misery for everyone, and parents often feel trapped and helpless. Because it is so commonplace for siblings to treat each other badly, and because people see other families struggling with the same dilemma, they assume it can't be escaped, but this is, again, another ridiculous assumption.

Good behavior among siblings can only occur within a family context of mutual respect. If you are raising your children to act impulsively and with little regard for others, how can they modulate the natural tendency toward sibling rivalry? Competition between siblings is entirely normal and something anyone with a brother or sister struggles with. We are all prone to jealousy and comparing ourselves to others, and the family is the stage on which we all portray our darkest selves. Everyone knows we tend to treat those closest to us the worst.

It takes awareness and a positive intention to mange one's most base tendencies if siblings are to overcome their disagreements in a constructive manner. This is the same struggle married couples face regularly. Many couples who come to me for therapy have difficulty understanding that it is possible to be angry – even furious – with their partner while controlling what they say or do. These patterns of communication are learned in childhood and practiced in our relationships with siblings.

Research shows that poor sibling relationships and mistreatment by a sibling can be as damaging to a child as a negative relationship with a parent. There is tremendous potential for sibling relationships to influence the kind of people our children become and the kind of intimate relationships they are capable of as adults. What if you could get your children to stop fighting, as well as increase the likelihood of their future happiness? Would you want to do it?

The first answer to the problem of fighting among brothers and sisters is for parents to change their expectations of their children. If you accept their bad behavior and bickering as normal, it will continue. If you decide you want peace in your house and are serious about it, it is possible to greatly reduce how much your kids fight and to improve how they behave when they aren't getting along. My general recommendation to parents is to go home and have a family meeting to discuss the issues of disrespect and squabbling, which must be directly addressed. Tell your children you are tired of all their fighting and that you want to live in a family where people treat each other like they care. This attitude should apply to all members of the family. If you are someone who screams at your kids when you're angry, your children will likely scream at each other too. Discuss setting a higher bar in terms of mutual respect and acting like a loving family. Be very specific about what won't be tolerated and create consequences to back it up. Don't let your kids call each other names or demean each other. **_Don't allow any physical aggression between your children_**. Be a model of what loving, tolerant behavior is and when you get angry, take the time to calm down so you don't say or do things you'll regret. When your kids fight, give one warning for them to stop. If they don't obey, administer previously agreed-upon consequences – and whatever you do, be consistent about it!

Sometimes children's fighting is a result of stress in the parents' marriage. Children are highly sensitive to tension between their parents. Often, the level of fighting in the household will reflect the status of the marital relationship. Fighting between you and your spouse will only make it more likely that your kids will fight too. If you are unhappy and have frequent disagreements in your marriage, do something to make things better. Get marital counseling if you need it. Creating more peace in your relationship with your partner will translate into more peace among everyone.

Stop accepting discord and disagreements as status quo for your family. You are entitled to expect more. My clients are often shocked by how little it takes to get their children to stop fighting like cats and dogs; it requires is commitment, consistent parenting, and often, tending to their marriage to make it happen.

Manners

In recent years, several books have been written about the loss of civility in American society. Old-fashioned notions about good manners seem to have dwindled away. Some children are raised learning to say "Please" and "Thank you." They are taught how to share and not take the kindness of others for granted. However, many children have not been taught these basic civilities. I can recall many times when my children's friends said nothing in response to considerations I extended, such as giving them a ride home or offering them a meal.

Why are manners important? Manners are a social enactment of kindness and consideration. When someone gives me something, I have a choice to appreciate their efforts or take them for granted. When I ask for something, I can expect it to be given to me just because I think I deserve it, or I can recognize that I'm expecting a person to go out of their way for me. My responses to another reflect my attitude about myself. If I've been raised to be given what I want when I want it, with no show of respect or gratitude, I will be an entitled person who thinks little about the feelings of others. I won't respect or regard others except as a means to getting my own needs met.

If I've been raised to speak to others in a polite way and appreciate what is given to me, I will grow up to appreciate the kindness of others and be empathic. I will have been raised with an attitude of respect.

I realize that what I'm describing should be self evident. It is shocking, however, to see how many kids haven't been taught these basic values. How can so many parents believe their children don't have to say "Please" and "Thank you" or treat others with kindness? It seems parents believe their children will somehow magically turn out to be well adjusted, caring adults, in spite of how unruly or rude they are as children.

For the sake of your child's social development, you must have appropriate expectations of them from the earliest ages. Teaching good manners and kindness should begin as soon as makes sense. By the time a child is three years old, they should already understand how to speak to others in a civilized way. That doesn't mean they will have the maturity or self control to always behave appropriately, but a baseline understanding of what is polite and what is rude should already be in place.

It is appropriate to expect your toddler to show consideration for other children and to learn how to share. This is more difficult for some children than for others. Parents of children who have trouble sharing have to work harder to teach the upside of kindness and the downside of possessiveness. Learning consideration for the needs of others shouldn't be optional.

Of course children model their parents when it comes to social behavior. If you are a person who displays good manners and respect for others, your child will mirror this. Studies have shown that children who show empathy toward peers are those who have been raised empathically. If you want your children to be polite and have good manners, work on relating to them in this way. Thank them when they give you something without making too much of a fuss about it. Instead of commanding them to give you something, ask with a "Please." If you model this behavior yourself and expect it from your kids in return, it is very likely you'll have the kind of children others admire.

One of the best compliments I've heard as a mother was "Your daughter is so polite." Another was "Your son shows so much appreciation." It is not that difficult to raise well mannered, respectful children if you are dedicated to making it happen. Be consistent with your expectations and show a combination of kindness and firmness. Your children will learn proper social behavior that will be reinforced by others. You will have the pleasure of hearing others speak well of your children. That sense of pride is worth all the work you will have put into teaching them.

False Praise

This is a pet peeve of mine and has been for many years. It has become commonplace for parents to praise their child's every effort and accomplishment, no matter how small. The phrase "Good job!" is something I hear parents saying to their children everywhere I go. This phrase seems to be used indiscriminately, from simply doing what a parent requests to an achievement of some consequence.

Since when does good parenting mean giving out accolades for almost any positive behavior? I believe this kind of praise has grown out of the cultural notion that the development of a child's self esteem depends on constant positive reinforcement by the parent. Of course our children want to know they're doing a good job, and naturally, they flourish in the face of appropriate approval. However, if we praise virtually everything they do, how can they discriminate between significant and insignificant accomplishments? The phrase "Good job" becomes meaningless when it is spoken too often, as is true with almost anything we hear.

Equally important is your child's ability to trust your assessment of them. If your child knows you are telling them things that are untrue, they will be less likely to trust what you have to say. On a gut level, children know everything they do is not special or deserving of praise. When we fawn over every accomplishment, our children know that we are lying to them. When we praise them too often, we dilute what a compliment actually has to offer. As is the case with money, praise needs to be earned. Children do better when praise is reserved for significant accomplishments or a true application of effort.

Indulging your child with excessive praise is really no different than indulging them with anything else; if overdone, it loses meaning. Rather than fulfilling a need, it creates a sense of emptiness. Truthful and appropriate praise will help them trust you and know themselves better, greatly increasingly the likelihood that they will develop a healthy level of self esteem.

An Honest Assessment

The parents who come to see me are usually quite frank about their children's problematic behaviors. There is little 'saving face' going on in my office, as they are usually at the end of their ropes by the time they step through my door. However, in life outside of my office, I generally notice that parents want to deny and/or rationalize their children's poor behaviors.

I vividly recall an experience from when my son was only three. I had taken him to a local pizza place, where they had an extensive play area for children. He was happily running about with all the other kids when he emerged from an enclosed area with a bloody nose. I was somewhat alarmed and asked him what had happened. He explained to me that an older girl had forcefully pushed him down, causing him to land on his face and get hurt. After tending to his injury, I asked if he could point out the girl who had done this to him. He said he could. I picked him up, and we proceeded to walk around the restaurant looking for her.

Without hesitation, he pointed out a girl who appeared to be eight or nine years old. I went up to her with my son and asked where her mother was. She had an immediate reaction of fear and guilt, clearly visible on her face. There was no question in my mind that my son had accurately identified his young attacker. The girl pointed to her mother, who I then approached. She was sitting and talking with another woman but quickly looked up when I addressed her.

I explained to the mother what had happened and how my son had identified her daughter as the person who had hurt him. Not surprisingly, the mother's immediate response was to deny that her daughter had done anything wrong. She said this without even looking at or speaking to her child. She attacked me for believing the word of a three-year-old and refused to discuss it further. And just like that, the conversation was over.

How can our children learn to take responsibility for their actions if they are not held accountable for them? As much as a parent might want to believe only the best about their offspring, all children and all human beings are flawed. It is our job as parents to face the truth of who our children are – the good, the bad, and the ugly – and love them for all of it. Contrary to popular opinion, it is not damaging to a person's self esteem to face their flaws. When someone already has a poor self image, they struggle with confronting anything negative in themselves. This is because any criticism is experienced as a validation of their poor self worth. If an individual has high self esteem, they are better able to tolerate appropriate criticism, as there isn't a need to see themselves as flawless.

It is also helpful to be honest about one's own flaws as a parent. How well do you know yourself? Do you know your strengths and weaknesses? Can you admit your personality or behavioral flaws to yourself and to your immediate family? In a loving family, there should be an overall tone of acceptance. Family members should have a fond tolerance of reasonable flaws in one another. Parents should be able to accept that they don't have perfect children and, in reality, shouldn't expect them.

Our children are not meant to be an extension of our own identities or a reflection of our worth. If our child acts out in a way that is offensive to us, it is our job to face that reality and take appropriate steps to remedy the situation. How can we teach proper behavior to our children if we won't face the truth about them? Surely it is sometimes easier to deny a difficult reality than to figure out what to do about it. When it comes to parenting, though, this is a luxury that we can't afford.

When other parents or teachers approached me with a problem they were having with one of my children, my initial reaction was to be open to what I was being told. Why? Because I had a realistic perspective of my kids' strengths and weaknesses, and I was typically not surprised by what I heard. I didn't need to create a more comfortable story for myself. I could then approach my child with an accepting attitude. I fully expected my children to be frank with me about what they had done and let them know their honesty was what I valued most. We could then have a straight forward conversation about what had happened and how to rectify the situation.

Some children are more willing to be honest about their misbehavior than others. I was always impressed with my son's unusual willingness to tell the truth about what he had done. Even in situations where he had seriously misbehaved, he would tell on himself, earning the nickname 'Mr. Honest'. Most children will hide from and frequently lie about their misconduct, but in my son's case, this was not the case.

Emphasize the importance of honesty to your children and model it as well. Try to put aside your need for perfection and face the truth that we are all a mixed bag of good and bad traits. Try to have a sense of humor about your flaws and own them openly. This will be an example to your children of self acceptance and accountability. It will make it easier for them to be honest with you and with themselves about their own bad behaviors and shortcomings. Don't overreact when your child does something wrong, as they need not be afraid of coming to you or taking responsibility for what they have done. We all make bad decisions in life and fall prey to our weaknesses, and it is the true test of our worth how we handle these incidents. Tolerate imperfection and don't expect your kids to be perfect as an extension of your own self worth.

Responsibility

As I listen to young adults in my practice, I frequently hear stories about the irresponsible behavior they see in their peers. Late teens and young adults have always had to struggle with entering adult life and all the responsibilities that transition entails. However, the problems I hear about today are somewhat shocking to me. The basic responsibilities of managing one's own time, finances, and surroundings seem to be beyond many, and in some cases, these present habitual problems.

I look back to my generation and don't remember young people having these kinds of difficulties in these kinds of numbers. That's not to say Baby Boomers didn't undertake their own share of acting out, terrible judgment, and irresponsible choices. However, I don't recall knowing many individuals who couldn't master the basics of adult life without their parents' assistance.

In previous generations, parents had different expectations of children. We and previous generations didn't have a choice about being self sufficient. It was expected that we'd become independent by our early twenties or sooner. Going back another generation, many children were expected to be working and helping support their families as early as their mid teens, having to sacrifice school attendance to help out at home.

It is true that maturation seems to be taking longer and longer. This generation of parents has had more time to devote to their children. Well-intended mothers and fathers spend large amounts of time driving their children from one activity to another, helping them get their homework done on a daily basis, allowing their children to sleep with them whenever they wish, and assigning their kids few chores, if any.

There seems to be confusion about where support ends and enabling dependency begins. The truth is, children need help managing their lives only until they are able to undertake tasks on their own. Too many parents allow themselves to get stuck in the role of doing things for their children that kids can and should do for themselves. Parents themselves often resist moving to the next level, which entails them stepping aside while offering encouragement. Because they have been so intertwined in their children's responsibilities, they come to believe their child doesn't possess the abilities to do things on their own. They begin to lack faith in their child's competence.

This lack of faith in one's child can become a self-fulfilling prophecy. A parent who fears the child can't function on their own inadvertently creates a dependent child. Even when parents are ready to encourage their child to move on, if they have allowed too much dependency for too long, the child will have diminished confidence in themselves. One can see how this problem can become circular in nature.

If you never expect your child to calm themselves down, be self-motivated, figure out solutions to their own problems, or act as a productive member of your household, how can your kids learn to do any of these things on their own? Surely, children need to be taught how to master these tasks, and it is the parents' role to teach them. Sometimes, however, the teaching never ends. Parents remain overly involved and mistrusting of their child's abilities and the child grows to depend on the parent to do anything that is the slightest bit difficult for them.

In this chapter, I will address the following developmental milestones, each part of the maturation into a responsible, capable adult:

- The ability to self regulate
- The capacity to self soothe
- Feeling independent enough to take on new tasks
- Time management skills
- Being accountable
- Becoming self motivated
- Feeling a sense of responsibility toward others

Self Regulation

Self regulation refers to an individual's ability to stay balanced in dealing with internal, as well as external challenges. *Regulation of affect*, defined as "the ability to modulate an observed emotional response," is essential for healthy psychological functioning. One must be able to regulate their own expression of emotions or they risk feeling overwhelmed and helpless. An inability to do so also affects one's social relationships. It's hard to be close to someone who gets overly upset whenever a problem arises.

The term also refers to one's capacity to be self regulating in coping with the challenges of daily life. Managing one's time, practicing proper sleeping and eating habits, and balancing work and play all require an inner sense of balance.

How does one learn self regulation? The experience of emotion begins at birth. Infants are born largely unable to self regulate. It is through natural maturation and environmental expectations that we develop the ability to control and express our emotions appropriately. As time passes, we also learn how to manage the daily requirements of life – or at least that's what's supposed to happen!

When you allow your child to scream at you, they are not learning how to express their frustration in a regulated manner. If they cry every time they face the smallest challenge, your child isn't learning how to put things in perspective – an ability that augments self regulation. When children are unable to control their emotions, they feel out of control internally.

Children need to be able to express their emotions, and the younger the child, the rawer that expression will be. It is the parents' job to teach the child mastery. Displaying empathy, talking and listening to your child, and letting them know you expect them to calm down sets the stage for the development of healthy self regulation. It is also absolutely essential for parents to display self control in order to teach self regulation. Children's expression of emotion is largely based on what they have observed in their families. A child who is raised in a family where everyone screams at each other will be likely to do the same. It is only through good modeling and having the expectation that your child can and should control themselves in an age appropriate manner that they will learn to do so.

Self Soothing

When I am upset, how do I get myself to calm down? I say soothing things to myself: "It's not that bad" or "It'll be okay." What do I do when I'm troubled and have difficulty falling asleep? I tell myself to relax, take deep breaths, and think about something pleasant. If I didn't have the ability to say these things to myself, I would likely remain agitated without reprieve.

Being able to soothe oneself is a wonderful thing. It's like having a kind parent living inside of us who comes to our aid when we lose perspective. People who lack the ability to self soothe truly suffer. Their feelings run them, and they are often overwhelmed. Self soothing is a skill which can be learned in adulthood, although not easily. One of the greatest gifts you can give your child is the ability to self soothe.

Some children are easy to soothe. When upset, they respond quickly to your efforts to calm them. When they cry, it's not protracted or overly distraught. Other children are more high strung and struggle with intense emotions. These children require more soothing by you over a longer period of time. However, the goal of teaching them to calm themselves should always be kept in mind.

Successful parenting involves helping your child make the transition from receiving your comfort to comforting themselves. But how, and when is this appropriate?

As I explained in the chapter on "Attachment," infants are not born with the ability to self soothe. They are entirely dependent on others to help them calm down. Our initial sympathetic bond with our baby is essential to their future ability to self soothe. By the time a baby is six months old, they have already internalized our soothing and are developing the ability to calm themselves.

An example of teaching a baby (older than six months) to self soothe could be offering them a favorite cuddly toy or blanket to help them calm down. Another example is comforting your baby initially when they awaken at night, followed by telling them to go back to sleep and leaving the room for a brief period. This gives the child an opportunity to attempt to calm down on their own while still knowing you have not abandoned them.

With older children, communication is key. Parents need to encourage children to talk about what is upsetting them, help them examine the situation, and include them in the search for possible solutions. It is also fine to sometimes offer solutions that the child can implement.

Talking about their distress helps the child (or anyone, for that matter) organize their thoughts and feelings and process them more fully. When a child can do this in the presence of a soothing adult, they learn that difficult feelings are manageable.

Helping children understand difficult situations and entertain possible solutions allows them to engage different parts of their brain while upset. Gaining a meta-perspective of a distressing situation can be quite calming.

As your child gets older, it becomes entirely appropriate for you to expect them to calm themselves down. Middle and high school-aged children can be told they need to calm down or at least work at making that happen. If upset enough, some kids will respond, "I can't calm down!" The parents' focus at that time needs to be helping their child find a way to make that happen. The importance of settling down when overly upset rather than communicating while overwhelmed is an important task to master. Your child's future life partners will thank you for it!

Sleep

Being able to fall and stay asleep requires self soothing. This is a very passionate topic for many parents. Therapists often struggle with parents over where, when, and how their children should sleep. This can be a topic of such disagreement that many parents leave therapy over it.

In more recent years, the idea of 'co-sleeping' or 'the family bed' has gained popularity. In many households, parents and children sleep together, sometimes without age limits. In my own practice, I have heard of teenagers who still get into bed with their parents when they are upset and sometimes even spend the whole night there.

I have mixed feelings about this topic, especially when it comes to babies and very young children. I can understand why mothers want their infants to sleep with them, although safety needs to be a major consideration. I can even accept this period of co-sleeping lasting into toddlerhood.

I am a strong believer, however, in children learning to sleep independently at an early age. The reasoning behind this is that sleeping is an activity children need to be able to master. Falling asleep, staying asleep, and handling distress during the night are things we must do throughout our lifetimes. There won't always be someone else in our bed to help us feel safe or calm.

If I saw evidence that sleeping with a parent increases feelings of security and self soothing and enhances a child's ability to sleep better in the long run, I'd be all for it. Unfortunately, this has not been my experience. Often, children who have been allowed to sleep with their parents long term don't learn adequate self soothing, or it is delayed significantly. In instances of long-standing co-sleeping, kids tend to be more regressed, less confident, and more dependent. I have even encountered cases of college-age young adults leaving school simply because they never learned how to sleep independently.

Many mothers complain to me of disrupted sleep and eventual exhaustion because of their child sleeping with them. When I suggest they get their child into his or her own bed, these mothers inevitably tell me how difficult that process would be. Many complain they are too tired to even try to make it happen. With my encouragement, parents do move forward and get their children to sleep independently; they are often surprised to find the struggle lasts only a couple of nights.

Some parents sleep with their children because it is a comfort to the parents themselves. I will repeat here what I said in an earlier chapter: ***If you are getting your own needs met rather than doing what is best for your child, you are failing your child.***

I am well aware that in some cultures, children sleep with their parents indefinitely. My own mother still talks to me about how in Eastern Europe, she shared a bed with her mother until she was twenty years old. Her brothers slept in the same room, in the same bed with their father. This was mostly due to the reality that there was only one bedroom to be shared between two adults and four children.

Children exist within the context of their culture. In America, the expectation is for children to become independent and function separately from their parents. This can mean living on their own in a college dorm or living across the country. Because we have that expectation, our children need to be raised to be more independent.

In discussing self soothing and independence, I am not in favor of leaving a child to feel lonely at night or at any other time. Parents can be available to their children when needed without sleeping with them. If your child crawls into your bed wanting comfort from a bad dream, I see nothing wrong with letting them stay until they are calm or asleep. Although it might be easier to let them remain with you until morning, I recommend getting up and taking your child back to their own bed. In this scenario, your child will benefit from your comfort and the experience of waking up in their own bed in the confidence-boosting knowledge that they got through the rest of the night on their own.

Feeling Independent Enough to Take on New Tasks

In order for children to gain a sense of competency, it is necessary for parents to foster their independence. Although this seems obvious, many parents undermine their child's development of a sense of competence by doing too much for them. Whether the parent has an actual lack of faith in their child or not, the child may grow to lack faith in themselves. Competence is gained by taking on something new, overcoming fear, practice, and eventual mastery. If parents don't allow and encourage their children to take on difficult and sometimes unnerving challenges (age appropriate and safe, of course), parents deprive their kids of the opportunity to prove themselves.

Later in life this can manifest itself as an adolescent's fear of trying something new, such as getting a driver's license, going to college, or living away from home. It can also cause your child problems in adapting to the natural changes that arise with growing up, such as moving from elementary to middle school or beginning to date.

If your child of any age claims they are unable to do something they haven't tried before, encourage them appropriately. Don't just take over and do the task yourself because it's easier or because you want to save your child any frustration. If you step in too much or too soon, your child will learn that giving up is an option.

Frustration is part of the learning curve. It needs to be tolerated while our will remains engaged. By allowing your child the freedom to take on new tasks, face their frustrations, and overcome them, you will be allowing them to experience success of their own making – an all-important and healthy life lesson. When appropriate, step aside and let your child learn on their own. They will be more independent and eventually able to face the challenges of adult life with an attitude of competency.

Being Responsible for One's Possessions

At what age should a parent expect their child to begin caring for their own possessions and environment? As soon as possible! Within reason, it is almost never too early to teach your child to have a sense of responsibility and respect for their possessions.

Toddlers tend to be high energy and create chaos wherever they go. Having the freedom to move and play freely is necessary for exploration and development. This doesn't mean you need to supply your child with a ridiculous number of toys in order for them to be stimulated. I will address the issue of materialism and toys later, in the chapter on "Play."

Some children have so many toys that it's virtually impossible for them to be in charge of cleaning up their mess. Many homes are so inundated with playthings that there isn't even room to store them all.

Making your child take responsibility for their own belongings starts with requiring your toddler to help you clean up their play messes. The child should do at least half of the work involved, within realistic limits. If you choose to give your child forty toys to play with, they are not going to be able to pick up twenty of them at the age of two!

Giving your child a reasonable number of toys and expecting them to put them away teaches your child ownership and responsibility. Many parents are tired by the end of the day and want things cleaned up as quickly as possible. Because of this, they often take over and clean everything themselves, expecting little or no help from their child. This is a mistake. I recommend building cleanup time into play time so your child will adapt to the routine of cleaning up after themselves.

As children get older, they need to learn both good organizational habits and a sense of value for their possessions. What do you do if your child loses something of value? Surely we all lose things from time to time. Children are more distractible and less organized, so they are more prone to losing or misplacing items. A certain amount of patience with this behavior is appropriate. However, as your child gets older, they need to be taught that with ownership comes responsibility. Automatically replacing a play thing your nine-year-old loses isn't necessary. It would be wiser to teach them to earn, save, and spend their own money to replace it. This will create in them a sense of value for their possessions and a desire to take better care of their belongings in the future.

Teens should be held responsible for their possessions, including clothing. I strongly encourage parents to have teens replace what they lose through irresponsibility. If your teen enjoys the extravagance of owning a car, make it their responsibility. If they damage it, they must earn the money to get it fixed. Teens should have to pay for some or all of their gas and car insurance. This makes the car theirs, not just a convenience item funded by Mom and Dad.

As for teaching your child to be responsible for their surroundings, include them (in age appropriate ways) in keeping the house orderly. I don't believe in having our children clean our houses for us, but they should be involved in some family effort to help keep things in order. This teaches ownership, pride, and some modicum of work ethic. It also teaches your child that they are not exempt from working at managing their environment.

Teenagers, in particular, are prone to having messy rooms. This is one area I believe parents need to have some tolerance for. That not withstanding, parents have the right to place limits on just how messy a teen's room gets. Disorder is one thing; dirt is another.

It is troubling to hear the number of complaints I get about the cleanliness (or lack thereof) of teens and young adults. Some of the stories I am told are outright disgusting: food left out to rot for days, trash not taken out for weeks, sidewalks so high with snow that mail can't be delivered, and these are only a few examples. This level of irresponsibility and lack of cleanliness appears to be becoming commonplace.

I find this very disturbing. It's as if these adolescents are waiting for someone else to come along and clean up after them because they have never learned to care for themselves. This is another example of entitled behavior that has largely been created by parents.

It is wise to incorporate your child as some part of the machinery that keeps things in order. In the next chapter, "Work," I will discuss specific age-appropriate expectations for your child. From taking out the trash to cleaning up their rooms, teach your children to value a decent living environment. If you are the only one making that happen while they're growing up, you may be creating an adult who thinks they are above such menial tasks.

Time Management Skills

Managing one's time well is something we can teach our kids from the beginning by setting eating, sleeping, and nap schedules. I realize modern life is hectic, and it's sometimes difficult to stick to these time frames, but I believe children begin to learn early on how to pace themselves and manage the ebb and flow of time.

Bedtime

Having a set bedtime is of utmost importance. Some parents have told me they allow their children to go to bed whenever they want. I think this is irresponsible and harmful to the child. Children almost always resist going to sleep, and if left to their own devices, they will stay up too late, only to pay the price the next day.

Having a predictable and preset bedtime is part of creating a structure for the day. It also ensures that your child gets enough sleep. When you tell your child, "It's time to get ready for bed," it forces them to focus on being organized and carrying out a routine by a certain hour. Through this, they will learn about setting limits on activity, as well as time management.

Homework

Homework is another area where specific time should be set aside. Having a daily routine of study time creates structure and predictability in a day. It's also more likely that your child will get their work done without it turning into a stressful battle. I've heard endless accounts of parents fighting with their kids to finish their homework well beyond what should have been bedtime. With younger children, it's appropriate to ask how much homework they have and be sure to set aside enough time for them to get it done in a timely fashion.

Unfortunately, the amount of homework assigned to even young children can sometimes be exorbitant. This has created more battles for parents, trying to get their kids to do work they feel overwhelmed by. Given the excessive amount of homework assigned by some teachers, it is even more necessary to create structured time in which to complete academic work.

Wakening

Another frequent area of conflict is getting up in the morning and out the door to school on time. The majority of parents who come to see me complain that their children don't want to get up on time in the morning. These parents are fed up with nagging, cajoling, and threatening. Some have asked me if it's okay to throw cold water on their resistant child. (And by the way, it isn't.)

Many parents have assumed the responsibility of their children getting up for school. Since when did it become a mother's job to argue for thirty minutes with a sleeping kid? I don't recall my parents or any others I knew getting their kids up for school. (The same could be said for parents helping with homework on a regular basis.)

Teach your child timely awakening by buying them an alarm clock and teaching them how to set it. Make it their responsibility to get up on time. Younger children may need more help. Communicate to them that it is their responsibility to become more self sufficient at getting themselves up as they get older.

With middle and high school-aged kids, missing a ride because they are late (even if you are the driver) means they have to find some other way to get themselves to school on time. I realize many parents are fearful of allowing their child to walk to school on their own, and in some situations, this simply may not be advisable. Common sense must prevail. If your child is unable to get to school independently, there should be a different consequence: Missing an after-school activity or having to do more work around the house are two possibilities.

Tardiness

Some teenagers refuse to get up on time in the morning and are chronically late to school. Chronic tardiness may result in loss of credit for classes. In severe and repetitive cases, a high school student's graduation may be jeopardized. Parents often panic at the thought that their child won't graduate on time.

Being late to school should not be accepted or excused by parents, except under unusual circumstances. Your child needs to suffer the consequences of detentions or loss of class credit in order to learn that lateness carries a high cost. Their future employers will thank you for teaching them this important lesson.

Parents sometimes get sucked into enabling their kids by keeping them from suffering these losses. They may excuse tardiness or race to get their teen to school on time. It is essential that you get out of your teenager's way and allow them to experience the natural consequences of their tardiness.

An important transition to adulthood involves being able to rely on oneself to get up and get to work on time. Managing one's sleep and waking times, along with accountability for tardiness, are essential to being a responsible employee. Being late or not even making it to work have become commonplace in young adults.

Help your children avoid this pitfall by making them accountable for their own time and schedules as soon as they are able. By learning self wakening and punctuality at an early age, they can be spared much failure in the future.

Being Accountable

In my work with couples, I always emphasize accountability as one of the most important elements of a good relationship. *Accountability* means, "I know myself. I can admit to my faults and take responsibility for my actions." Realizing what we have done wrong and owning up to it builds trust and hope in an intimate relationship, and this is why healing in intimate relationships begins with accountability.

Children need to be held accountable for their actions, as well as the impact of their behavior on others. Young children tend to want to blame others for what they have done. They may deny blame even when they are caught red handed.

As a parent, you need to be firm in your conviction that your child takes responsibility for what they have done wrong. This can be done without shaming or frightening them. Within the family, a standard of honesty needs to exist that all members are expected to adhere to. This standard needs to be taught and reinforced consistently.

You can set the stage for accountability by displaying it yourself, including with your child. It is appropriate and good modeling to own up to your own mistakes and apologize. This doesn't mean you are on the same level with your child; apologizing to them doesn't make you any less of an authority. It is simply a way to display common courtesy and respect, which any person deserves.

Start talking to your child about their behavior and how it makes others feel as soon as they are able to understand this concept. These kinds of discussions should be educational, not guilt inducing. Your goal should be to teach your child kindness and empathy. Not doing so can create a narcissist, someone who is unable to see others clearly.

Reinforce the idea that everyone makes mistakes and reward your child when they show a conscience about what they've done wrong. By not shaming them, you teach them that all people have flaws and that shortcomings don't define us. Being accountable will lead to better self esteem, as doing the right thing builds self esteem, even when it's a difficult undertaking.

Becoming Self Motivated

Temperament plays a role in how self motivating a person is. To a certain extent, this is an inborn trait. What parents expect and how they follow through on those expectations can have an enormous impact on their child, regardless of temperament.

In psychological literature, there has been a longstanding debate about nature vs. nurture. Over the years thinking has swung form one end of the spectrum to the other. Recent studies have shown that the effects of one's inherent nature vs. the manner in which they are raised carry equal weight in determining what kind of person one becomes. This means the treatment of our children has an enormous effect on who they will be.

All children have to learn a certain amount of self motivation. For those who are inherently driven, parents need only assist with new challenges as they arise. Even compliant kids will face developmental tasks that they'd rather avoid. It's the parent's job to encourage independence by expecting their child to challenge themselves.

With children who tend to avoid or hold back from taking on responsibilities, parents need to express their expectation that every person is in charge of his or her own life. Too often, parents become the motivators for their children, fearing that if they stop their child will fail. We all learn through trial and error, and failure (error) is part of that equation. If you remind your child again and again to do homework and they resist, preferring to entertain themselves, you are putting yourself in the role of being their motivator.

It is more helpful to remind your child of the consequences of their inaction and allow them to rise to the occasion of their own tasks. We all have to learn to make ourselves do things we don't really want to do. It's the threat of possible negative consequences that sometimes has to motivate us, even as adults.

Feeling a Sense of Responsibility Toward Others

The increase in narcissism among young people is indicative of their sense of disconnection from others. If I've been raised to focus primarily on my own pleasure and needs being met, I likely will have inadequate awareness of the needs of others.

Again, we can look to our culture and see how this attitude has caused us to deteriorate on many levels. The current financial crisis we are in stems largely from narcissism and greed. The people on Wall Street who were looking to make as much profit as they could at the expense of others behaved in a narcissistic manner. Clearly, they didn't feel a sense of responsibility to those who were being affected by their self-aggrandizing choices. Our country is in shock that so many could have behaved without conscience or a sense of responsibility toward others.

In order for us to develop a culture that displays the values of relatedness, social responsibility, and an overall sense of community, we need to work at raising our children differently. Parents need to teach that we are not put on this planet only to indulge our own desires or to achieve as much success as possible, but to feel a sense of responsibility for the wellbeing of others.

This is not the same as assuming responsibility for someone who won't do so for themselves. Ultimately, each person is responsible for their own lives and choices. The flipside of that coin is that we are all human beings who, at one time or another, will need and appreciate the help of others. Feeling an appropriate sense of responsibility for others means we are aware of those around us and tuned in to what another person might need. We must feel a sense of connection to others.

This past winter was a tough one in Michigan – cold and snowy. I was in the parking lot of a market in my small town, struggling to maneuver my grocery cart through the accumulating snow. Next to my car, I saw two elderly women trying to shove their cart through cement parking bumpers. I went over and asked if I could help by carrying their bags to the trunk of their car. They refused, but I just went ahead and did it anyway. One woman turned to me and said, "You are exceptional! No one has ever done that before. Thank you!" to which I replied, "If I'm exceptional, we're in a very sad state of affairs." It was disturbing to me to think that had I driven away, no one else would have helped them. Have things really gotten that bad?

We need to emphasize kindness and an awareness of others when it comes to raising our children. This is the antithesis of too much of what I see in my office: kids overly focused on their own entertainment and pleasure with an emphasis on materialism and financial success. I have literally had to explain to many of my young clients that money is not what brings happiness. They look confused and surprised when I quote statistics that show that wealthy people are often the most depressed.

From the time your child is old enough to be aware of the feelings of others, encourage them to share and have compassion. Explain that we are here to look out for one another, asking them how they would feel if they needed help and no one responded. Giving your child a sense of interconnectedness with others will greatly contribute to their happiness throughout life and cause them to feel less lonely and depressed as they mature.

Work

It was only two generations ago that it would have seemed absurd for a psychologist to talk to parents about the need for children to work in order to develop an appropriate sense of responsibility. In times passed, children were expected to function as part of a family unit that had to work in order to survive. Most of us have heard stories from family members who grew up in the first half of the twentieth century. Back then, many young teens had to quit school because their parents needed them to earn a wage to help the family get by. Others had to quit school to work on family farms or in family businesses. Self-satisfaction was not an issue, as survival and responsibility to one's family had to come first.

It is kind of shocking to think of the lives of children in the past as compared to what is expected of children today. In my private practice, it is entirely commonplace for parents to tell me their late teen has never had a job of any kind. Some young adults graduate from college never having worked, even during summer breaks. I also hear stories of college-aged adults who live with their parents and don't go to school or work. Do these parents think they're doing their adult children a favor by allowing them to be completely dependent and nonproductive?

A disturbing trend I see in my office are teens and young adults expressing an extreme distaste for work of any kind. When I talk to them about earning their own money or the inherent satisfaction one gets from being financially independent, they tend to stare blankly at me. Typical answers I hear in response to my questions about what they want from life are: "I want to be rich"; "I want to have as little responsibility as possible"; "I want a really nice house"; and so on. They are usually shocked when I explain that being wealthy does not equate to happiness and that in fact, the incidence of depression among the wealthy is quite high.

It feels strange to have to explain to so many young people that happiness comes from good relationships, working toward a goal, having a supportive social network, and believing in something greater than oneself. I sometimes feel like I am teaching the most rudimentary facts of life to people on the brink of adulthood. I would compare it to teaching an eighteen-year-old how to divide and multiply during their last summer prior to entering college. How can it be that children are growing into their teens and twenties without any understanding of work and autonomy as a central aspect of life?

The following is a prime example from my practice of a young adult from my practice who lacked self-direction or any sense of what would make her adult life satisfying:

Anita was a bright, attractive, twenty-five-year-old woman who came to me with a history of depression, cutting, and highly dependent, unsatisfying relationships with men. She was in graduate school studying engineering. Anita came from a family of enormous wealth and, as such, had never needed to work. She'd had jobs but didn't keep them for very long, even though she was a motivated and good worker.

In her treatment, Anita struggled in a profound way with what the purpose of her life was. She stated she didn't enjoy work. "It's boring," she said, "and what's the point?" She and her wealthy peers preferred to spend their time shopping, buying things she knew she didn't need. Although Anita had contempt for this lifestyle, she couldn't figure out what else she was supposed to do. She sometimes expressed a fantasy of being one of the salesgirls who waited on her at the mall.

Therapy was challenging for Anita. She was acutely aware that she had an enviable life by most standards. She could buy and do anything she wished; however, Anita struggled with intense feelings of loneliness and emptiness. Defining her purpose, setting goals, and working to achieve them were much more difficult for her than for most of the people who come to me for treatment.

In session, we had long conversations about having a more grounded life, which included work and self sufficiency. Although I could explain the need for this on a theoretical basis, it was hard to convince someone that sticking with mundane tasks and earning meager money would bring her greater happiness. Wouldn't we all rather not do a tedious job but be handed money instead?

Anita had been robbed of the opportunity to learn about the value of work. Her parents' financial support to the point of indulgence hadn't allowed her to develop an appreciation for hard work and the personal evolution that comes with it. Starting a new job is frightening; mastering it, learning to work with others, and becoming increasingly proficient are wonderful rewards. Anita had never experienced any of this, and this was part of the reason her life felt so meaningless. She was truly one of the most desperate and lost young people I had ever seen in my office.

It's easy to see how children of wealthy families are overindulged and not expected to work. However, I have seen this phenomenon in all social classes. I know of families who struggle financially, barely earning enough to get by, while their grown children still live at home and don't or won't work or contribute any money to the household. These young adults are living in a fantasy created and supported by their parents. Even worse, they are also missing out on developing the necessary emotional maturity and job skills that will afford them a successful adult life.

An additional aspect of emotional development derived from tedious or unchallenging work is something that psychologists refer to as 'being in the flow'. This is the experience of transcending the task at hand and entering an observing, peaceful state of mind. When one is 'in the flow', time passes more quickly and we are able to fall into the rhythm and meaning of everyday tasks. There is a gentle, gradual movement of thought that takes us outside of ourselves and allows us to perform tasks in a somewhat meditative state.

What percentage of our lives do we spend performing repetitive, mundane tasks? Even for those of us fortunate enough to have lives that allow us to think and act creatively, most of life is about the mundane. Learning to work and develop an attitude of tolerance for ordinary tasks is essential to a sense of ease and even pleasure in everyday life. Without it, life can feel empty and meaningless. This is some of what I addressed in the first chapter of this book: Increasing numbers of children and young adults feel empty and have difficulty attributing meaning to their lives.

Developing an appropriate sense of responsibility and diligence, a good work ethic, and an appreciation for the value of money all require one to work!

At what age should you expect your child to start working? As soon as they are able to start picking up after themselves. Doing a good job will teach your child the inherent satisfaction of being a productive person. If you cater to your child, do everything for them, or give them money whenever they want it, you will deprive them of that sense of accomplishment.

Earning Privileges

The concept that your child earns their privileges is one that sets a tone of working for – rather than being entitled to – what one receives. It is antithetical to the notion, "I deserve to be given whatever I want just because of who I am." This is the essence of entitlement, which sets the stage for the development of narcissism:

"I am special. Life should give me what I want, and I shouldn't have to struggle in the process. If I'm struggling, it's someone else's fault."

A child's development of a world concept is overwhelmingly derived from their experience in their own family. If I grow up in a kind and loving household, I'll develop the belief that the world is a beneficial place. If I grow up abused and neglected, I'll perceive life to be about deprivation and pain. There are a few exceptions to this, of course, such as the unusual individual who grows up in a stressful environment, yet maintains a sense of optimism.

Much of what goes on in adult therapy is the exploration and understanding of the formation of our world concept and its inherent distortions, which are projected onto and often reenacted in our lives. Clearing up these distortions and realizing that the past is over can free us up in remarkable ways.

The development of either a sense of entitlement or one of responsibility and gratitude are largely determined by how a child is raised. If a child is treated as if every tiny accomplishment is worthy of accolades, in addition to having all of their needs met without work or challenge, the chances are high that they will grow up to be self-centered. A person only learns about the notion of earning something by being put in that position.

When your child has to earn privileges, they learn both how to work for what they want and how to appreciate what they are given. Everyone knows working for something is more gratifying than just having it handed to you. When children are freely given all gifts, opportunities, and privileges without working for them, they miss out on this inherent pleasure.

I am not implying that every single freedom or opportunity your child is given needs to be earned. It is one of the great pleasures of parenthood to give your child experiences or possessions that make them happy. However, requiring your child to finish their chores before allowing them to go out and have fun, or earning a special privilege by having to meet realistic expectations is an essential part of parenting a responsible child.

Handing everything to your child because you take pleasure in their happiness of the moment is about your own satisfaction, rather than building strong character in your child. Once again, *if you are indulging your own need for pleasure and/or closeness with your child rather than teaching them, you are failing in your role as their parent.* It is your job to teach your children that work is an essential part of life and that rewards are a result of one's own efforts.

It is common for me to hear stories of clients giving their children extraordinary opportunities, even when these same kids are underperforming dramatically in school or behaving disrespectfully at home. Some examples I have seen are teens with bad grades and terrible study habits who get sent on overseas class trips; elementary age children who refuse to be cooperative at home, yet get expensive videogame systems; and middle school pre-teens who refuse to get ready for school on time in the morning, but have a car full of peers and a parent waiting for them every day. These examples are so commonplace and so often overlooked that parents reading this may be surprised that I consider them overindulgences of children who are not being taught to earn what they are given.

How can young people learn that good and bad consequences are the result of their own efforts? As an adult, they won't have the luxury of showing up late or performing poorly at a job while still getting bonuses and accolades. If they don't learn to behave responsibly and work hard, how will they get the money to take the trips or get the things they want when they are grown?

In the field of psychology, it has been understood for over a century that what makes life worth living is love and work. If we deprive our children of the opportunity to work, we deprive them of the gratification and emotional development that can only be derived from their own efforts. No parent can give a child the sense of accomplishment and competence they achieve through their own labor. As loving and generous parents, we naturally desire to make life easier and more pleasant for our children in every way. However, good parenting involves allowing our children to struggle and to develop and eventually master all of the elements required in adult life. Work allows one to feel a sense of purpose and responsibility, which is undeniably necessary for successful adulthood.

Expect your children to pick up after themselves, to complete age-appropriate chores, and to work for others to earn spending money when they are old enough to do so. Don't shy away from expecting your child to contribute to the work involved in running your home or from doing some forms of physical labor. Have your child work side by side with you and teach them to be conscientious about what they do. Expect your children to assume responsibility for getting their own homework done.

Of course good judgment needs to be used by parents when determining what an appropriate task is for their child. Talking to other parents you admire or even consulting a professional can be very helpful in setting new guidelines for discipline, expectations, and limit setting. I often meet parents who struggle with setting new boundaries for their children because they are surrounded by other parents who are equally lost. A one-time consultation with a professional can be extremely helpful in getting parents on the right track. Many parents have come to see me only once or twice, seeking guidance for managing their children. Sometimes all parents require is an objective professional to validate their concerns and provide a sense of direction. You are not a failure as a mother or father if you can't figure it out by yourself

Play

The topic of children and play is one near and dear to my heart. This is probably because I am a playful person myself. I find playing with children to be a joy, whether in my office as part of their therapy or in my private life. I love the opportunities play allows for communication, spontaneity, and expression.

As parents, we begin to see the first inklings of what our children's preferences and abilities are by watching them play, even as infants. What makes our child laugh? What engages their interest? We watch them struggle with physical development and frustration tolerance as they master the use of a toy or puzzle. We see the joy they experience from something that tickles them, something particular to only them.

I have such sweet memories of my son as a baby, and one of them was the way he always laughed in response to the sound of me running my finger down the mini-blinds in his room. He also laughed with abandon when I sang "Take Me Out to the Ballgame." Through my play with him, we developed a more loving bond based on fun and mutual pleasure. I learned about his idiosyncrasies and preferences. I watched him master new skills and eventually venture into the world of play with others and all the social pain and pleasure that entails.

Childhood should be an essential time in our lives for freedom, creativity, exploration, and expansiveness. Childhood play allows for the development of personal interest and preferences, interaction with nature, social relationships, physical development, opening oneself to new possibilities by joining in play with others, exploration of the arts, and other endless possibilities. It is through play that children express themselves and join with others.

In playing alone, a child learns about mental stimulation arising from one's own imagination. There is the time and space to let one's thoughts run free and to experience pleasure and curiosity. The roots of personal creativity are fostered in childhood as children get to explore what captures their interest. Only the limits of their own imagination get in the way of new ideas, actions, and pleasure. A child left to their own devices can make a toy out of almost anything and take enjoyment in the simplest activities. I think of my daughter as a little girl, spending hours in her room creating worlds and creatures out of paper clips, stones, cotton balls, and anything else she could find. I always had to walk through her space carefully and respectfully, trying not to disrupt all of her meaningful creations.

I also recall her 'cooking' with play dough or preparing imaginary 'tea'. So much concentration went into her play! It always amazed me that after all her work, she was satisfied with me pretending to quickly gobble up what she'd made for me. It was obvious how much joy she took in the act of creation and mimicry.

Playing with others allows us to learn about social order, cooperation, sharing, and how to be part of a team. We even learn how to cope with the pain of being the last person chosen as a playmate. Our earliest learning about personal politics comes from play with others. A child will learn about kindness by identifying with a peer who's being left out. They will learn to share, fighting against instinctual selfishness. They will learn about personal power and how to use it or abuse it. They will learn to answer the questions: "Am I popular or avoided? Which of my behaviors draw people toward me, and which push them away?" Through play with others, children gain a sense of how they are perceived outside of their family circle. They may, as a result, be encouraged to learn new skills and take new risks in order to fit in. Play leads to challenges in the areas of individuation and development of personal judgment. A child who plays learns how to be their own person and make their own decisions as a consequence of playing with others.

Whether it's playing alone in one's bedroom or in a neighborhood ball game, play is essential to normal personal, social, physical, and mental development. Our brains are built for stimulation and growth through childhood play. Across all cultures and throughout history, children have found ways to have fun through physical activity, social interaction, and personal exploration. I take note of this in my psychotherapy practice: Virtually every client I've ever met recalls what kind of play they enjoyed as a child, describing fondly their absorption in various activities with others or alone. Even people with difficult or starkly lonely childhoods will describe to me their childhood imaginings and play that brought them fulfillment and made their lives tolerable. This includes those who grew up in poverty. Children with little or no access to commercial goods are not limited in how much they enjoy play. They simply find ways to create fun from whatever resources they have available. A child can create a whole world out of paperclips and cotton balls, and it is important to encourage them to explore healthy play.

Toys

As a young child born in the 1950s, my life was filled with play. Until I was age six, my family lived in an apartment building in Newark, New Jersey. Like some of our neighbors, my parents were immigrants, and no one in the neighborhood had much money. Most of my play was outdoors, running around the neighborhood and playing imaginary games with my friends. On Sunday mornings, my sister and I played in our bedroom, allowing our parents uninterrupted time to sleep in. We often pretended we were camping, creating a makeshift tent out of a collapsible TV stand, putting it on our bed and throwing a blanket over it. Toilet paper mixed with water and stirred in a pot was our food. This play was absorbing and fun. I couldn't have cared less what implements we were using; it was all about what we created. Most children I knew didn't have many toys – not even the babies I knew, except for an occasional rattle or teething ring.

When I got a little older, we moved to our own home in a suburb. The most significant gift my parents ever gave me was a brand new piano for my sixth birthday. I had begged for a piano for over a year, and they were incredibly generous in this gift to me. The piano became the center of much of my free time. I took lessons and played for many years. I easily recall the range of my feelings as I learned to play, struggling with difficult pieces and lost in the music, exploring all the sound that could be produced, even opening the top of the console and playing the strings inside. I loved playing piano and never had to be told to practice. It allowed me expression of so much emotion and a sense of mastery that was extremely meaningful to me, from my initial lesson onward. I felt so proud when I learned to read my first notes and translate them into what my fingers played on the keyboard.

During my elementary school years, I received a Barbie doll, along with a few outfits for her. Like many girls, I enjoyed dressing her and imagining different scenarios for her. Sometimes, a friend would bring her doll over and we'd play with them on mirrored coffee tables in my living room, pretending they were dancing in a beautiful ballroom. Again it was all about what we could create within our social scenarios, practicing adult life through our play.

Although I grew up in a middle class home surrounded by successful families, most of my peers had very few toys. I knew one girl who was an exception, as she owned many extravagant playthings. We all thought of her as spoiled, but we also envied her and tried to be invited over as much as possible.

In the 1950s and 1960s, toys were seen as a supplement to and not the source of play. Peer play, physical activity, and creativity were the basis of childhood fun.

Fast forward to life in the new millennium, and the significance of toys has exploded. Take a walk into the homes of most young children today and you will see a plethora of playthings, a virtual treasure trove of toys. With the exception of significantly impoverished households, most families have more toys than their children could ever play with. Often, there is an entire room filled with toys. Parents complain that it takes so long each day just to pick up all the toys that they sometimes elect not to do it.

Materialism in childhood has become the order of the day for even the youngest children. Children expect toys to be given to them from their peers at birthday parties and from family members at holidays. Parents fight with other parents in stores to purchase the 'hot item' toy for their child. Large amounts of money are spent on specialty dolls, videogames, motorized vehicles, and on and on. Children's desire for toys is satiated even when the family has limited means.

Many parents have bought into the notion that being a good parent means meeting all of their child's material longings. If their child wants an iPod or the newest game system, they feel it is their responsibility to provide these items and thereby avoid disappointing their little one. This kind of child rearing will lead to identification with materialism as the answer to happiness and greatly increases the likelihood of raising a narcissistic child.

If a child is surrounded by adults who give them excessive material goods and are motivated by guilt or social competition, the child doesn't learn how to tolerate disappointment. The child develops a belief that their wants are paramount and should be met by others without delay. This places their needs at the center of the universe and doesn't allow for identification with those who are doing the giving.

If a little boy wants a computer game and his parents go to the local toy store to immediately buy it for him, what does he learn? He learns that his wishes are gratified upon request and don't require sacrifice by another person. He builds a paradigm of the world in which the universe and everyone in it exists solely to meet his needs without frustration. His own sense of importance becomes over-blown, and he perceives that his needs should be met simply because he exists. He will consider that he gets a toy not because he has earned it in some way or learned to wait until his parents have the money, but simply because he is who he is and wants what he wants.

This is the definition of *entitlement*: "I am owed by law or privilege certain rights." When a person is given what they want whenever they want, they naturally develop a belief that it is owed to them. Human beings are extremely adaptable, and it doesn't take much for us to develop expectations that are unrealistic and even self-destructive.

If that same little boy wants a computer game and his parents explain to him that such a toy is expensive, requiring work and time to acquire, he learns to wait for what he wants and develops an appreciation of the efforts put into obtaining it. Most importantly, he develops the concept of delayed gratification, which is key to emotional intelligence.

In my office, it is very troubling to see so many young people seduced by the false belief that material goods will bring them happiness. As a self-proclaimed aging ex-hippie, it amazes me to see the younger generation falling into this trap. Having name brand clothes, the most expensive purses, or the fastest and most up-to-date computer is something I frequently hear younger clients discuss. I even saw one client in her twenties who stated that although her husband was a responsible professional, because he didn't aspire to earn enough money to give her what she deemed 'a good life' (which included very specific, extravagant items), she didn't think she wanted to bother making the marriage work.

This is an example of another downfall to giving children too many things: They begin to equate love and inner fulfillment with the acquisition of goods. Research shows again and again that being wealthy and having all one wishes for is not what brings people happiness. It is social connection, purposeful work, and spiritual faith that bring the most meaning to life.

Some parents get caught up in the social competition of making sure their children have as much as their peers. They fall for the pressure their kids exert on them, falling prey to urgent pleas: "Everyone I know has a cell phone!" or "All of my friends have cars!"

What is expected of parents to 'keep up with the Joneses' has gotten completely out of whack. From buying babies every possible stimulating device to buying a sixteen-year-old a car (and then paying for the gas and insurance for them), parents have become slaves to their children's material demands.

Again it is important to look at this phenomenon in the context of our current culture. Children are not the only ones who expect their material demands to be satisfied without delay and without sacrifice. Our current economic crisis is rooted in overindulgence and living beyond our means. People with limited funds buy flat-screen TVs and homes they can't afford, living on credit. Immediate gratification and a lack of planning for the future have become the norm, the American way of life. Adults are losing homes, jobs, and all their savings as a result of our years of mismanaged finances and self-indulgence.

This economic crisis has been lauded as a time to get back to reality and learn to live within our means. Could it also be a time to teach our children that wanting something doesn't mean getting it without patience and hard work? The time is right for our culture and our children to move away from materialism and toward a more grounded, internally motivated manner of functioning. This means living without things we can't afford or don't need.

As a parent, you get to decide what is right for your own child. The issue of materialism is no different than any other parental issue. It is your responsibility to instill good values in your children. Whether it's teaching your child to be kind to others or instilling in them the value of work or money, you – and not your culture – should be the primary influence on your child.

As a parent, do you have the guts to put your foot down and not indulge your child's material wishes, even if it means giving them less than their peers? Can you feel like a good mother or father if you don't have piles of unused toys lying around like everyone else you know? Can you trust your child to have the ability to create their own play through imagination and inventiveness? It takes a strong person to stand up to societal pressure and 'pack mentality'. As a parent you get to choose how you want to raise your children, even if it flies in the face of what those around you are doing. Just because every single one of your child's peers has a cell phone or videogame system or iPod doesn't mean you have to provide your child with the same.

Children will pressure their parents and sometimes express feelings of deprivation if they don't have all the things their friends have. As a parent, you must be strong enough to make your own evaluations about what you feel is best for your child, even when it comes to toys and entertainment. If you don't want to raise a child who believes that materialism brings happiness, stop indulging their materialism! Modulate how much they are given.

As a society, we are beginning to see and pay the price for the overindulgence of children. Being able to say "No" is an essential part of being a good parent, and learning to accept "No" as a child is just as important for the development of a civilized, empathic human being.

Extracurricular Activities

Virtually all of the children who come to see me have significant involvement in extracurricular activities such as sports, music lessons, religious school, scouting, and others. Families often place great importance on these activities, centering their lives on practice schedules and spending a lot of time driving from one event to another. When I strongly advise parents to start eating family dinners together on a regular basis to promote greater communication and closeness, they inevitably tell me it's not possible because of all of their children's commitments. Meals frequently involve eating fast food in the car as they drive from soccer practice to basketball practice. It's not unusual for a child to come into my nibbling on fries and chicken nuggets during the session because there isn't any other time in the day for dinner. Even scheduling a therapy appointment becomes challenging because of the priority parents place on all of their children's extracurricular commitments.

There is no doubt as to the value of involvement in team sports for a child of any age. From physical fitness to good self esteem to developing the capacity to work well with others, participation in team sports is of great benefit to children. However, I have seen the role of children's involvement in sports change drastically in the past ten to fifteen years. Too often, family life and the majority of their free time are centered on their child's team schedules. In my practice, I frequently notice that entire family lives revolve around the child's sports involvement. Whole weekends are spent driving long distances from one game to another with families sometimes staying in hotels to accommodate all-star games and playoffs and tournaments. The siblings of these children frequently complain to me that they feel less important than their brother or sister who seems to be the center of their family life. I have never seen an instance where any of these children were being groomed for professional career as an athlete. Rather, their abilities and their parent's belief that they must do all they can for their child too often create a profound emphasis on the importance of sports in general, regardless of the consequences to the rest of the family.

Like issues involving sleep, parents are often quite resistant to being told their child's schedule needs to be altered. Parents balk at making any changes, even when children complain to me that they have too much to do and not enough free time and that they actually want to give up a sport or lesson to have more freedom. The parent often purports that their child *needs* all of these activities in order to become a well-rounded person. When I explain, "In fact, excessive activities are harmful to a child, not allowing open time that is essential to good functioning," parents still refuse to remove their kids from any activities.

I believe these parents are caught up in a sense of guilt and competition and have bought into a culture of excess and indulgence. Your child does not need to be trained, taught, and proficient at multiple skills in order to be well adjusted. When a family's life revolves primarily around a child's recreational schedule, it can communicate that the child is the center of the universe. On the flipside, it can communicate that the parents' need for the child to excel is more important than the child's wellbeing. It is important for parents to consider the impact on all family members when deciding how much involvement their children should have in extracurricular activities, rather than assuming they must afford them every opportunity.

The most intense session I've ever had with a child had to do with exactly this issue of extracurricular activities. Many years ago, Sandy, a boy of nine, was brought to me by his divorced mother because of social difficulties and a general sullen nature. Sandy's relationship with both of his parents wasn't very good. His father was an older man from another culture, whose expectations of Sandy were out of date and inflexible. Sandy's mother was very attached to his younger sister, but she was somewhat cold and rejecting of Sandy, mostly because he reminded her of her ex-husband.

After many months of seeing Sandy in therapy with little progress, he came into session one day saying he wanted to quit violin lessons. He'd been studying violin for several years but didn't want to continue. I suggested we bring his mother in and present his request to her. Sandy thought a joint session was a bad idea, but I persisted. It turned out that Sandy was right and I was wrong. His mother was completely close minded to this suggestion. In fact, she was fairly cold about it, even when he became tearful when she told him he could not quit playing violin. He became so upset that I had to ask his mother to leave the session, and it took another forty minutes to calm him down. I was quite concerned about him for the next week, and I called his mother to check up on how he was doing, as I'd never seen him so distraught and inconsolable.

Much to my amazement, Sandy returned to therapy the following week a different person. I had never seen such a dramatic shift in a child's behavior and personality. His unengaged and lackadaisical attitude was gone, and he now related to me in a warmer, more personable, more normal manner. These changes generalized to his relationships with peers, and he became a happier and more responsive child. Only a couple of months later, his mother withdrew him from treatment. I called a couple of times to keep in contact, and for several years, I wondered how he fared after I stopped seeing him. It is my belief that the dramatic change in Sandy was a result of a situation that allowed him to attach more deeply to me in the therapy following the profound pain and disappointment he experienced with his mother in session.

In my practice, I have never seen a child who suffered or expressed regret for giving up an extracurricular activity by their own choice. In fact, I frequently hear children say they are too busy and wish they had more free time. Children often complain that they feel pressured by their parents in this regard and are frequently met with resistance if they discuss cutting back on extracurricular activities. Although parents may start out involving their children in sports and lessons for the child's own good, they seem to get lost in the excessive involvement our culture promotes. Limit your child to three extracurricular activities, including religious school, and scouting. In my opinion, one sport at a time is enough for any child, although I understand that for many families, this is not the case. If your child excels at a sport and is involved in a traveling team, there should be even fewer than two additional activities. Find a balance between committed activities and down time. Stop buying into the notion that your child has to excel at everything. Stop looking at what other people are doing and give your child the free time that all children deserve. The result will be a calmer child, more family time, and improved relationships among siblings.

Technology and Media

This is a topic I could probably write an entire book about. There seems to be an endless parade of parents marching through my office saying, "I can't get my kid off the computer!" or "All my son/daughter wants to do is play video games!" When I ask what the 'screen time' limit is for their child, the answer is usually, "We don't have one."

Most of these same parents lament about the differences between how they spent their free time as children (playing outdoors with others) and how their own children are often inactive and solitary in their play. It is obvious to me that today's parents feel they cannot stem the tide of their offspring's degree of involvement with technology as a form of play.

Children's access to technology has, in many cases, become all consuming. From movies playing on screens in the back of minivans to hand held videogames, kids seem to be inundated with the over- stimulating effects of technology.

I fully appreciate the reality that our world has changed from one where personal computers didn't exist to one where being computer literate is essential to successful functioning. I also understand the importance of children having commonly held interests that foster social connection and a sense of belonging. Whether it is playing video or computer games with others or talking about a popular movie or TV show with friends, shared interests and experiences help children find their place in social groups. This allows for a common understanding, which is at the root of all friendship.

Technology and virtual play are here to stay, but how much your child indulges in this kind of stimulation is up to you. The average amount of time children now spend either on computers, playing videogames, or watching TV is seven hours a day. That amount of time spent away from others and disengaged from the real world cannot be good for anyone. Our brains, bodies, and nervous systems were not designed for sitting in front of a screen fifty hours a week.

The problems I see in my work with children's access to technology are multifold:

- ***Computer and videogames are addictive***
- Virtual play removes one from the real world
- Our brains adapt quickly to the hyper-stimulation of gaming and are no longer satisfied with the natural pace of real life
- Personality changes such as irritability, impatience, and withdrawal
- A tremendous increase in power struggles between parents and children
- Longer term and serious deficits in social aptitude
- An over-emphasis on personal gratification and a lack of identification with work and effort
- Depression and poor self esteem
- The decline of physical fitness and all the concomitant illnesses
- Lack of creativity
- Shortening of the attention span

The greatest problem I see with virtual play is that it removes one from the real world and involvement with others while creating an unnatural state of internal stimulation. A slow paced game of kickball with one's neighborhood friends cannot match the rapid firing of brain neurons that occur in a computer or videogame. Video games are designed to create a sense of challenge and excitement that real life cannot live up to except under extraordinary circumstances. In real life, external occurrences are sometimes routine and boring. Even team sports involve a flow of excitation and downtime. Real- life play requires a child to be patient as they wait for their teammate or opponent to take their turn. Parts of our play are exciting, while other parts are routine. The child learns about the ebb and flow of energy and excitation in active play with others, but this is not the case with technical games. There is ultra-rapid stimulation which keeps a child hyper-focused on and involved with the game. After a while, this level of arousal begins to feel normal. The dull pace of real life can never keep up.

Another danger of gaming is a preoccupation with fantasy, encouraged by long periods of time living in an alternate reality. I am strongly opposed to any gaming that involves violence, particularly first-person shooter games. What good can possibly come of a child getting lost in a world where they wield weapons and mass destruction is depicted? What has our society become when we even entertain the notion that this is an acceptable form of play?

There is a lot of debate about whether violent virtual gaming leads to increased acting out of violence by children, but the answer to this should not even require research. It should be common sense that exposure to violence can't be good for children. These games exist because we are vulnerable to the stimulation of our most primitive drives. Sex and violence are mainstream in media and entertainment because they are commercially successful. Our brains are excited by exposure to sexual and/or violent images. That doesn't mean we need to be exposed to them in excess as adults or that our children should be exposed to them until they mature.

Parents need to be strong enough to use their own judgment about matters such as how much violent or sexual material their child is exposed to, regardless of what anyone else is doing. Take a moment and think about the reality that so many children live each day: They spend their free time alone in a room, the company of other people replaced by an alternate reality that allows them to act out heir worst violent fantasies. Can that possibly be the basis for sound psychological and physical development? The honest answer is a resounding "No."

Other types of play foster aspects of personal evolution: creativity, cooperation, sharing, physical development, and an appreciation of nature and materials. Virtual games do not develop any of these, and sitting in front of a television or a computer monitor can never replace the value of real-life experiences in the real world. Add to this the social isolation that occurs when a child sits in their house playing by themselves, and you may begin to understand my grave concern about technological play.

My recommendations for how to manage your child's exposure to computer and/or videogames are simple, although they require patience, commitment, and consistent effort on your part if they are to be enforced. These include:

- Limit your child's screen time.
- Monitor and control what your child is exposed to.
- Implement and follow through with consequences when your child breaks these rules.

How much time should a child be allowed to spend in front of a screen each day? This depends upon your child's age and level of development. Young children use virtual games strictly for entertainment, while older children and teens also use computers for social networking. Although it's not unusual for children to spend many hours each day on a computer or playing a videogame, I would recommend no more than one hour of play for young children and no more than two hours for older kids and teens. Even these limits are higher than I would like them to be, and I strongly support allowing even less time in front of the screen.

I personally raised my children with no more than one hour of television daily until they were in middle school. Excessive use of videogames was not allowed, and my son consequentially lost the use of his gaming system for months at a time because he had difficulty moderating his use. I wasn't willing to have ongoing power struggles about something as meaningless as a videogame. When I realized this was detracting from his overall ability to relate normally, the games were taken away.

Enforcing limits and consequences was sometimes very trying and time consuming. I often had to disconnect the keyboard and mouse from the computer and take them with me as my only means of ensuring limits. My husband even installed a removable plug for the television set so we could control how much time our kids spent in front of it when we weren't home. We also didn't subscribe to cable television programming until our oldest was in high school.

Why did I go to such lengths to limit my kids' exposure to media? My son has since told me I was unusual in my parenting because I allowed him so much freedom in areas most parents don't: the freedom to explore, to make his own decisions, to try new things. At the same time, I didn't allow what most parents do: unmonitored exposure to technology and media. Both of my children understood my limits were so strict because of my belief that excessive and unmonitored television and videogames have a negative effect on brain development. They knew the healthy development of their minds, intellects, and emotions was my top priority. I was willing to take time to play with them and expose them to new experiences rather than have them entertain themselves with technology. This doesn't mean I overindulged my kids, neglecting my own adult responsibilities to keep them stimulated. Playing with them, going fun places together, and providing them with the materials to explore their own interests were balanced with running my private practice and household. As a result, I saw my children develop the abilities to enjoy reading, music, alone time, and play with others. Technology was not the mainstay of their lives. I am proud of the talents and abilities they developed as a result of a low-tech upbringing.

Media

Like technology, our children's access to all forms of media – from cable television to music on the radio – is abundant. We are all aware there is too much sex and violence on TV, in movies, and even in song lyrics. Our taste for stimulation of our most primitive drives, sex and aggression, has been overindulged, and the content of our media is an expression of this.

It is our job to limit our children's access to media. I realize this is tremendously challenging in today's world, yet what makes it challenging is also what makes it a necessity. Young children are not meant to view sexual or violent images, and many psychological experiments bear the results of doing so: Children exposed to images of violence become more aggressive, and children exposed to sexual images become hyper-stimulated and are more prone to acting out sexually.

It is not unusual for a child who has seen pornographic images to want to act them out in some way, sometimes involving other children. When a child acts as a sexual perpetrator, the first thing psychologists look for is evidence of sexual abuse. Second to that, we look for the possibility of the child's exposure to sexually explicit material. Sometimes a parent in the house or an older sibling allows a younger child to view inappropriate sexual images. Pornography is easily accessible via cable channels or pay-per-view. Exposing your child to this kind of stimulation is considered a form of sexual abuse, as it involves sexual arousal as a result of an elder's actions. It is your job as a parent to ensure that your child has no access to adult channels on television or to pornography on the Internet.

On a lighter note, parents often dismiss the content ratings of television and film and allow their children to watch media with maturity ratings beyond those recommended for their child's age. The ratings exist for a reason, and I firmly believe parents should adhere to them. Your child won't be harmed if they have to wait until they are thirteen years old to watch a PG-13 movie. If you choose to have a young child watch a PG film, it is your job to watch it with them and to explain or clarify what they are seeing. Too often, parents plant a kid in front of a television set, turn on a movie, and walk away, oftentimes not even knowing the full content of what their children are watching.

Do not allow your children to have television sets in their bedrooms! This basic recommendation has been made by the American Academy of Pediatrics, yet the overwhelming majority of parents still allow it. Even with preset restrictions on programming, your child will be exposed to material that is inappropriate and potentially traumatizing. Fortunately, there are filters that allow us to limit our children's access, but they aren't extensive enough to do the job for us. Satellite and cable companies are not commissioned to raise and put limits on our children; that is our job. If we are going to have cable TV, we need to set controls on what our children watch via technology and personal involvement. It's almost a fulltime job to monitor everything your child sees and hears in the media, but it is part of being a responsible, loving parent.

We need to enforce the recommendations on music, film, and television ratings. We also need to inform the parents of our children's friends what our limits are when our kids are visiting. I recall numerous conversations I had to have in these situations when parents allowed my child to watch inappropriate television shows and movies at their homes. Those conversations were very uncomfortable because they implied that I disapproved of someone else's parenting decisions. On one occasion, a parent responded with anger and bashed me to my own child (who later told me about it!). Often, I had to make the request more than once. These negative responses by parents were an expression of disregard for my authority as a parent, and although it would have been easier to just give in and allow my kid to watch whatever they wanted to at friends' homes, I wasn't willing to make that compromise. What my children were exposed to was very important to me, and I was willing to put myself in an uncomfortable position – repeatedly, if necessary – to enforce what I believed to be good parenting.

One option is to simply not have cable TV in your home. This may seem drastic to most people, but it is a reasonable and responsible choice. I chose not to have cable television until my youngest child was twelve years old. My kids were raised mostly on public TV, and even then in limited doses. We watched and enjoyed programs together but spent most of our free time doing other things.

I know parents often use TV as a convenient babysitter, and I am not completely opposed to taking time to get things done while your child is engaged by an educational, healthy, or safely entertaining program. My recommendation is that television time be limited, much like my recommendation for technology, to one to two hours daily and that parents be fully aware of and responsible for what their children are exposed to. This involves ongoing work as a parent, but the consequences of not doing so are significant. Be a responsible parent and don't sidestep this awesome responsibility.

Adult Children

These are terrible economic times to become an autonomous adult. The unemployment rate among recent college graduates is staggering. Many young adults are finding themselves in a situation where they don't even have a choice about living on their own. It seems to be the new norm that young men and women graduate, only to move back home while they attempt to find work and save money.

The main problem I see with adult children not living independently is a delay in emotional emancipation from parents. Childhood becomes prolonged, even into adulthood. It is commonplace for college students to take five or more years simply to complete a bachelor's degree. In my practice, I have seen individuals into their later twenties living as if they are still teenagers. It can only be with the financial and emotional support of their parents that young adults remain dependent. Here are some examples of cases I have seen within the last few years:

A twenty-five-year-old woman still in undergraduate school whose education continued to be funded by her parents. She came into session with her mother, angry that her parents had not helped her find an apartment within walking distance of her school. She had put off looking for a place until one month prior to the beginning of classes. This young woman stated she refused to learn how to drive, had no interest in it, and didn't believe it was necessary. She lived in an area with poor public transportation. I watched as she treated her mother with contempt while the mother struggled to reason with her.

A twenty-seven-year-old man whose housing and undergraduate education were being entirely paid for by his parents. He and three other young men all lived in a home owned by his parents and paid extremely low rent. My client complained frequently about his roommates, ranging in age from their late twenties to early thirties, having no motivation to do the most basic care of the home, interior or exterior. He claimed they spent endless hours playing videogames. He told me a story about the mail being undeliverable in the winter because there was so much unshoveled snow that their mailbox couldn't be reached.

A nineteen-year-old young woman who left college and moved back in with her parents, showing no motivation to work. Her parents couldn't understand my insistence that their daughter be productive and earn her own way as a means of developing a sense of competency. In session, they cited her involvement in various hobbies as an adequate way to spend her time.

Unfortunately, these cases are not unusual. From neighbors, colleagues, and friends I hear endless stories about young adults with the maturity of middle school children. This includes people in their twenties spending inordinate amounts of time playing videogames (to the point of causing serious damage to their hands), being evicted from apartments, getting fired from jobs, and/or simply being unmotivated to figure out what to do with their lives. Recently, a client told me about her brother, a thirty-one-year-old who works part-time and had his income secretly supplemented by his mother. The parents see no problem with his work life.

There is a difference between unavailability of work and a serious lack in motivation to find work. Since it has become culturally acceptable to live with one's parents after finishing college, the necessity to earn one's own way has also diminished.

The biggest problem I see with this current trend is a dramatic increase in feelings of incompetence and fear amongst young adults.

Having not moved forward into their adult lives, they begin to fear that they don't have what it takes to do so. Their emotional immaturity makes them less likely to have successful intimate relationships, and their choice of career is sometimes delayed.

There would have been a time when I would recommend to parents that they not allow their adult children to live with them except under extraordinary circumstances, but this is no longer the case. The reality of our economy is such that we are reverting to older constructs where multiple generations live within the same home. Problems occur when young adults continue to be treated as they were when they were teens or children and not as the adults they have become.

If your adult child is living with you, they should be held to adult standards. That means they should be expected to work fulltime and contribute financially to the family. Paying rent is entirely appropriate and should be expected. Even if your adult child is saving money to become independent, they need to pay you some amount of money on a monthly basis. This establishes them as adults who are expected to be self supporting.

While your adult child is looking for work, they should also be required to help with the upkeep of the home. Even if one of the parents has historically been the one to keep house, once a child becomes an adult they should be expected to help with household chores and errands every day if they are sharing the home with their parents.

How many adults get to live a life that doesn't involve work of any kind? Not many. If you allow your adult child to live with you and do no work of any kind, what are you teaching them? They will begin to believe the false assumption that adult life is about complete and utter freedom and does not require work because somehow, someone else will always meet their every need. They will feel entitled to the life you provide instead of working to make a life of their own.

Many parents my age complain to me of adult children who move out on their own, only to return home again and again. This is not always motivated by financial constraints. Sometimes a parent's willingness to support their adult child affords that child the unhealthy choice of leaving a job they don't like or allows excessive freedoms that are counteractive to responsible adult life.

I will never forget my first year out of college back in 1976. There was a bad economic recession at that time that I wasn't even aware of. I chose to move out of state and had to find housing in a competitive market. Finding work was even harder. There were few jobs available, and the competition to get any job was fierce. I ended up living in a house I didn't like with people I didn't care for, employed at the most miserable job of my life. It was a very difficult year for me. Eventually, I found a better job and moved to a better living arrangement. A few months later, I moved to a different state and found housing and work that I actually enjoyed.

I learned a lot in that first year, even though it was one of the worst years of my life. I learned I can find work under very trying circumstances. I learned I can manage on my own. I learned to live on very little money. Perhaps most importantly, I learned I am strong enough to get through tough times and make my life better. I got a better idea of what I did and didn't want to do with my life socially and professionally. I learned about the realities of adult life.

Had moving home been a comfortable and easy choice at that time, I probably would have made that decision. It would have alleviated a lot of suffering and anxiety, but in the process, it also would have delayed my maturation. My current ability to feel comfortable taking on almost any challenge was partly developed by those trying years. I know I can live almost anywhere, work almost any job, and survive on minimal finances if I have to.

Had my parents allowed me a cushy life where I didn't have to work or support myself, I surely would not be the confident and capable person I am today. The sense of competence I feel as an individual and even as a professional comes, in part, from my struggle to become a mature adult. It wasn't easy for me and there were times I was frightened and unsure if I could do it. It's only in the doing of it that I learned what I was capable of.

Don't deprive your child of the opportunity to take on life's challenges. They need to know you are there to support them as a backup if everything falls apart. Short of that, I encourage parents to push their adult children toward independence. Expect them to work. Expect them to contribute. Expect them to live independently and to confront their fears. Virtually any psychologist or psychotherapist will tell you the only way to overcome a fear is to face it, and it is no different for our children.

In loving your child, you may feel a strong pull to save them from struggle and anxiety, but there is no other way to create strength. The self confidence your child will develop from facing their fears and establishing their own successful life is ten times more valuable than having a safe haven they can retreat to and hide in.

It is possible to be a loving, supportive parent without being an enabler. Believe in your adult child's ability to be self sufficient, and they will begin to believe in it as well. Let them know you have confidence in them. Don't be overly anxious about the challenges they have to face. Past generations moved out into their adult lives because they didn't have a choice. It's the nature of life that we move from dependency to autonomy, from our primary bond with our parents to independence and later to an adult intimate relationship.

Let your adult child grow up and move into the life they deserve to have. Encourage them, listen when they want to talk, and give advice or guidance when needed. Don't abandon them in times of real need. Look realistically at what your adult child can do and expect them to do

Gratitude

Gratitude is, in many ways, the antithesis of entitlement. An 'attitude of gratitude' is an antidote for narcissism, in that it promotes a sense of humility and appreciation of others. This is the opposite of the narcissist's tendency toward self-aggrandizement and a lack of identification with anyone beyond the self.

Feeling grateful implies experiencing life in an open fashion, with our focus being outward while able to take in all that is good around us. There is a decreased preoccupation with the self and a greater sense of connection with the world. Our inner lives are enriched when we feel grateful, and our personal ties flourish as we appreciate what others have to offer. Exploitation of others for our own benefit, lack of empathy, and feelings of inner emptiness all fall away as we tune into the deeper positive aspects of our relationships and surroundings.

In recent years, there has been a lot of discussion in our culture about the concept of gratitude and how it contributes to our physical and emotional wellbeing. Studies have shown that individuals who focus on what they have to be grateful for are happier and healthier than the general public. Self help books and television personalities promote writing gratitude journals as part of an overall emphasis on positive psychology.

As is the case with empathy, children will absorb and model their parents' gratefulness or lack thereof. On the contrary, an entitled parent will likely raise an entitled child. As our economy struggles to recover and many people learn to live with less, we are offered an opportunity to develop a more normal range of wants and a deeper appreciation of what we have. The insanity of excess has caused many adults to feel unfulfilled as they get caught up in the cycle of working to buy things they don't need, possessions that will not bring true happiness and satisfaction. Many people have bought into the lie that more is better and are raising their children with that same empty notion.

Much of what I've written in this book has been about what not to do in order to parent effectively. Specifically, don't overindulge your child's material needs. We can only be grateful for that which we can focus on. If you give your child a ridiculous number of toys, it is obvious gratitude for any one gift will be diminished.

Don't allow them to be emotionally exploitive of you or anyone else. Expect respectful behavior at all times and teach them to identify with the feelings of others. Ask your child to put themselves in someone else's place and imagine what they would feel.

Don't encourage excessive dependency. Whenever possible and age appropriate, allow your child to take on their own responsibilities and offer them help if they need it. Don't assume they can't manage on their own.

Don't treat your child as if they are the center of the universe. Giving them huge accolades for the simplest accomplishments or telling them they are better than other people is a lie that will only cause them to mistrust you and be uncertain of who they are. A strong sense of self is built upon realistic feedback and grounded in true self knowledge. We all have inherent strengths and weaknesses, and it is not helpful to tell your child everything about them is wonderful.

As adults, we can set an intention to focus on the positive, feeling grateful for all that is good in our lives. How do we promote this world view in our children?

Do hold your child to high standards in the areas of kindness toward others, responsibility for the self, and appreciation for all you give them. A sense of appreciation begins with teaching your child to be grateful for what they are given from the earliest ages and by saying "Thank you" when they are helpful to you and expecting them give thanks in return. Something as simple as expecting thanks creates the understanding that one is not entitled but needs to reflect upon what is being given to them with a sense of appreciation.

Teach your children the connection between work and acquiring goods. When possible, allow them opportunities to earn what they are being given. Educate them about the cost of things and be sure they comprehend that someone is working to earn that money. There should be an understanding that material goods are the result of someone's effort, and gratitude for that effort should be implicit.

In teaching your children to be grateful and responsible, you will equip them with the tools to create a meaningful life. It is through our sense of accomplishment and connection with others that our eyes are opened to all the world has to offer. Whether getting a paycheck at the end of a hard week's work, walking through a forest, or sharing a meal with a friend, it is by being present to oneself and another that life takes on meaning. When I feel good about what I have done and grateful for what others do for me, I become enriched with a sense of satisfaction. No amount of praise or possessions can replace this.

When we decide to become parents we take on an enormous responsibility, as well as being the recipients of a tremendous gift. Being responsible and grateful are inherent in being a good parent. Pass these qualities on to your children by parenting them effectively and by having the strength to do what is right for them. In the end, their development of appropriate values and an ability to enjoy life will be worth a lifetime of effort. Children raised with an attitude of respect and gratitude will have the tools to feel good about the gifts in their own lives.

Notes

About the Author

Sheri Moskowitz Noga has a Masters degree in Humanistic and Clinical Psychology and is an EMDR practitioner. She has been in private practice for over thirty years working with individuals, couples and families. Sheri lives with her husband and near her two adult children in a suburb of Detroit, Michigan.

WHAT IS EMDR?

In this book, I have not mentioned EMDR as a treatment modality but described myself as an "EMDR practitioner". I want to share with my reader information about this exceptional tool which has allowed thousands of individuals to resolve past traumas.

"EMDR" stands for Eye Movement Desensitization and Reprocessing. It is a process discovered by Francine Shapiro, PhD, wherein eye movements are paired with the cognitive, emotional and physiological processing of traumatic memories. EMDR has long been recognized as an effective treatment for Post Traumatic Stress Disorder, but can also be helpful in treating anxiety, depression, unresolved grief and a multitude of other difficulties.

It is only within the last eleven years of my practice that I have done EMDR with clients. I was skeptical when first hearing about it and had my doubts when attended trainings. However, I have seen this very natural, non-intrusive method allow many of my clients remarkable results including resolution and integration. In my own practice, I have witnessed many individuals successfully processing memories that have plagued them their entire lives

EMDR is a powerful tool. I recommend that anyone interested in EMDR therapy for themselves or their child seek out a certified practitioner with a good amount of clinical experience. To learn more about EMDR or to find a list of certified practitioners, visit their website at www.emdr.com.

6431547R0

Made in the USA
Charleston, SC
24 October 2010